Native Americans' Pennsylvania

Daniel K. Richter

Pennsylvania History Studies Series, No. 28
The Pennsylvania Historical Association
University Park, Pennsylvania
2005

COVER: Ninth-grade classroom, Carlisle Indian Industrial School, 1901.
Cumberland County Historical Society, Carlisle, Pa.

Copyright 2005
Pennsylvania Historical Association
University Park, Pennsylvania 16802
ISBN 1-932304-37-1

Printed by
Huggins Printing Company
2900 Sycamore Street
Harrisburg PA 17111

Contents

Editor's Introduction

With this volume, the Pennsylvania History Studies Series remedies one of its most glaring omissions. For far too long, the series had no volume on Pennsylvania's first inhabitants. This longstanding void now has been filled with a most impressive contribution by Daniel K. Richter.

Dr. Richter is a noted scholar and an elegant writer, and it is hard to imagine anyone better suited to the daunting task of telling the story of Native Americans and Pennsylvania. That story is told here carefully, clearly, with due attention to all its inherent complexities and the many gaps in historians' knowledge.

Just as important, Dr. Richter reminds us that the history of Native Americans in the Commonwealth did not end two centuries ago—that, as he says, it is "a story that neither began with William Penn nor ended with the Paxton Boys." So the story as told here includes not only the expected figures and events—Teedyuscung, Neolin, Cornplanter, Penn, the Conestoga Massacre—but also the Meadowcroft Rockshelter, Paleo-Indians, the last Ice Age, the Carlisle Indian Industrial Training School, the "Indian New Deal" of the 1930s, the Kinzua Dam, and the recent resurgence of Powwows as a way of expressing a Pan-Indian identity.

This is, in short, a story of breathtaking scope, filled with drama, courage, and sometimes betrayal: the story of a people who were for millennia the only Pennsylvanians, and whose histories are inextricably entwined with the histories of those latecomers who eventually found their way to a "new" world.

Gary L. Bailey
Indiana University of Pennsylvania

Author's Note

John W. Larner provided an extremely detailed (and witty) reading of an early draft of the manuscript and improved it in countless ways. Brian P. Luskey provided invaluable research assistance. Amy Baxter-Bellamy, as always, gave unmeasurable practical and moral support. As editor of the Pennsylvania History Series, Gary Bailey patiently shepherded a long-overdue work to publication. I owe them all a deep debt of gratitude.

Numerous people and institutions eased the complicated task of tracking down illustrations and maps: Pierce Bounds (Dickinson College); Valerie Brewer (the Chicago Historical Society); Robert Cox (the American Philosophical Society); Sean Daily (the Newberry Library); Susan Dianni (the Philadelphia *Daily News*); Susan Drinan (the Atwater Kent Museum of Philadelphia); Stephanie Grace and Peter Potter (the Pennsylvania State University Press); Adrienne Gruver; Elizabeth Hamilton (the College of Physicians of Philadelphia); Laurence Hauptman; Barbara Katus (Pennsylvania Academy of Fine Arts); Barbara Landis; Charlene Peacock (the Library Company of Philadelphia); Kerry McLaughlin (The Historical Society of Pennsylvania); Janine Pollock (the Free Library of Philadelphia); John Pollack (University of Pennsylvania Libraries); Diane Reed, Mike Sherbon, and Brenda Wetzel (Pennsylvania Historical and Museum Commission); Richard Tritt (the Cumberland County Historical Society); Lucy Williams (University of Pennsylvania Museum); Jill Reichenbach (the New York Historical Society); Pat Virgil (the Buffalo and Erie County Historical Society); and Catherine Wert.

Chapters 1-3 are revised and condensed from Daniel K. Richter, "The First Pennsylvanians," in Randall M. Miller and William Pencak, eds., *Pennsylvania: A History of the Commonwealth* (University Park: Pennsylvania State University Press, 2002), 3-45. Permission to re-use this material is gratefully acknowledged.

Source footnotes are provided for only for direct quotations. To enhance readability, spelling, punctuation, and italicization have been modernized and abbreviations expanded in all quotations from works written before 1800.

Introduction

Perhaps the first image of Pennsylvania Native Americans that comes to mind is of William Penn's legendary treaty of 1682. Immortalized in Benjamin West's 1771 artistic masterpiece—which shows well-dressed Quakers exchanging trade goods with fascinated Indians in front of anachronistic brick buildings—and spread through dozens of variations by the early nineteenth-century Quaker artist Edward Hicks, the scene is deeply ingrained in popular culture. Although no documentation confirms that the precise event portrayed actually happened, the image conveys a certain truth. Infused with its Founder's personal vision and the Quaker values of many early colonists, Pennsylvania enjoyed remarkably peaceful relationships with its Native neighbors for more than half a century.

Benjamin West, *Penn's Treaty with the Indians*, 1771. *Courtesy of the Pennsylvania Academy of the Fine Arts, Philadelphia.* Gift of Mrs. Sarah Harrison (The Joseph Harrison, Jr. Collection).

But a second image then comes forcibly to mind. This, thankfully, was never romanticized on canvas, but it nonetheless is seared into the national consciousness, and conscience. Just before dawn on December 14, 1763, a militia from Paxton township burned the tiny Indian village at Conestoga Manor to the ground and murdered the six people who were sleeping there. Fourteen residents who survived were given refuge in the Lancaster city workhouse. Within a few days, a white mob broke in and massacred them all, leaving behind a gruesome scene of severed hands and feet, smashed skulls, and lifted scalps.

The two apparently irreconcilable scenes share a deeper connection than we might expect. The Conestogas—a small group of varied Native backgrounds—lived on a manor the Penn family had allotted them in 1718. Among the village's smoldering ruins lay wampum belts and papers recording a treaty with William Penn in 1701, along with the body of an elderly Seneca Iroquois man named Sheehays who was probably present for the signing.

Against this backdrop of tragically opposed scenes—of peaceful founding and brutal ending—a third, ill-formed but no less powerful, image also sticks in the popular imagination. There are no Indians in modern Pennsylvania, that image insists; their story ended sometime around 1763 and can now only be told in the past tense. This notion finds apparent confirmation in the 2000 U.S. Census. Among all fifty states and the District of Columbia, Pennsylvania ranks last in the percentage of its population that identifies itself as Native American—a mere 0.01%, compared to a national average of 0.90% and an average among the original thirteen states of about 0.04%. Moreover, among the original states, only Pennsylvania lacks both an Indian reservation within its boundaries and (as of this writing) any Native groups that have won legal recognition of their status from state or Federal governments. Clearly, it would seem, the vision of peaceful coexistence conveyed by the paintings of West and Hicks went tragically astray. Or, perhaps Hicks got it right after all. Most of his portrayals of Penn's Treaty were part of larger compositions depicting a longed-for *Peaceable Kingdom* where the lion would lie down with the lamb and a little child would lead all creation to salvation. Peace between Indians and Pennsylvanians lay beyond the secular nineteenth-century history that Hicks experienced.

But just as clearly as the first image of Penn's Treaty retreats into myth in the brutal light of Conestoga, the third image—that there are no Indians in modern Pennsylvania—is not literally accurate; 0.01% is not zero, and that statistic represents 18,348 living Pennsylvanians who in 2000 identified their sole race as "American Indian or Alaska Native." If those who place themselves in more than one racial category are included, the number expands to

52,650, or 0.4% of the state's population. A small proportion, true, in a total population of over 12,000,000, but hardly insignificant.

*   *   *

Yet neither numbers nor popular images can capture the human story of Native Americans in what is today known as Pennsylvania. Perhaps if we think less in terms of "Pennsylvania's Indians" and more in terms of Pennsylvania as Native people experienced it—a "Native Americans' Pennsylvania"—we can begin to glimpse a story that neither began with William Penn nor ended with the Paxton Boys, a story that began thousands of years ago and is far from over now. This small book traces some outlines of that story.

Edward Hicks, *The Peaceable Kingdom*, c. 1833. *Courtesy of the Pennsylvania Academy of the Fine Arts, Philadelphia.* John S. Phillips bequest, by exchange (acquired from the PMA, originally the 1950 bequest of Lisa Norris Elkins).

Chapter 1
Native Origins, to 1000

No one knows for sure when people first set foot on the land that, thousands of years later, English newcomers would call "Pennsylvania." But one thing is certain. People lived there for so many millennia that, for all intents and purposes, it could be called "forever." They were there even as the landscape itself took shape.

*   *   *

"Pennsylvania," as an irreverent historian once put it, "is a construction made by lawyers."[1] Its artificial boundaries bear little relationship to natural features or to any spatial order that humans might logically have created upon the land. Not surprisingly, then, modern state lines have little to do with the boundaries that Native people created for themselves over the millennia. Yet anyone who spends time in the modern state also knows that an enduring human geography does lie within the artificial lines. Eastern, central, and western Pennsylvania sometimes seem so ethnically, culturally, and politically different as to be separate states. As political strategist James Carville famously, if unfairly, put it, "Pennsylvania was always Philadelphia and Pittsburgh with Alabama in between."[2] The three-part division is more a product of geography than politics; three great river systems—the Delaware in the east, the Susquehanna in the center, and the Allegheny, Monongahela, and Ohio in the west—along with the low but nonetheless formidable barriers of the Appalachian chain define distinct geographic zones that, until the advent of railroads and modern superhighways, remained disconnected. To this day, once one leaves the Interstate, travel across the valleys and ridges of "the Endless Mountains" remains difficult. It has been so for millenia.

With some oversimplification, the three great river systems can be seen as a massive drainage system for the meltwaters produced by the glacial ice that covered much of northern Pennsylvania during the last ice age, which reached its peak in approximately 16,000 B.C.E.. The water trapped in all that ice lowered the sea as much as three hundred feet. As a result, the mid-Atlantic shore lay two hundred miles farther east than it does today, and the Delaware and Chesapeake bays did not exist; in their places were freshwater river valleys. The extended coastline meant that the portion of Pennsylvania not cov-

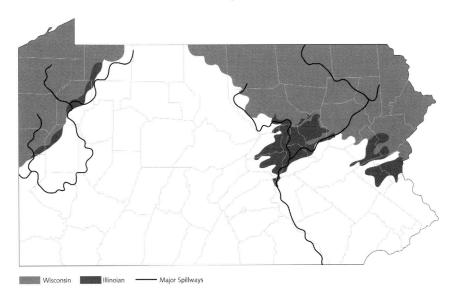

Glaciation in Pennsylvania, with major spillways that created the state's river systems. Randall M. Miller and William Pencak, eds., *Pennsylvania: A History of the Commonwealth* (University Park: The Pennsylvania State University Press, 2002), p. 5. *Copyright 2002 by the Pennsylvania State University. Reproduced by permission of the publisher.*

ered by ice lay far inland and had an inhospitably cold climate. Coastal areas would have been more welcoming to human settlement. So it is possible that evidence of the mid-Atlantic region's earliest population now lies beneath the sea.

Remains from a site approximately thirty miles southwest of Pittsburgh known as the Meadowcroft Rockshelter, however, demonstrate conclusively that some people lived within the present-day boundaries of Pennsylvania during the closing years of the last ice age. Controversy swirls around the dating of the stone artifacts found there, but, with a probable age of perhaps 14,000 years, they provide some of the oldest firm evidence of human occupation anywhere south of Alaska.

By 10,600 B.C.E., the glaciers had retreated from all of present-day Pennsylvania. For over two thousand years, however, the northern portion of the region remained a frigid, virtually uninhabitable, tundra. Farther south was a mixture of fir and spruce forests and open grasslands roamed by small herds of mastodon, mammoth, muskox, and caribou, along with larger populations of deer, elk, and moose. Areas near the seacoast (which remained far to the east of its present location) were a mixture of evergreens and leafy forests, wetlands, and open glades. These would have provided a rich variety of animal and plant resources for the human inhabitants archaeologists have traditionally called "Paleo-Indians."

Paleo-Indians left behind very different kinds of stone artifacts than did those who much earlier camped at Meadowcroft Rockshelter. Most distinctive were their fluted spear points—two- to four-inch spearheads with a groove chipped on each side to accommodate a split shaft. Because these and a few stone tools are virtually the only surviving evidence of the Paleo-Indians'

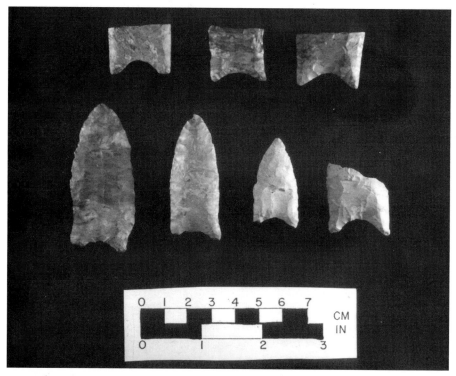

Paleo-Indian fluted points. These spearheads, notable for the groove chipped in each side to fit a wooden shaft, are among the few surviving pieces of evidence about the people who lived in what is now Pennsylvania more than ten thousand years ago. *The Pennsylvania Historical and Museum Commission, Harrisburg.*

existence, it is difficult to say anything definitive about who they were, how they made their living, how their societies were organized, or what differences in languages, beliefs, or customs may have divided them. Yet, far from being the loutish cavemen of popular imagination, Paleo-Indians needed complex skills to survive in their harsh environment. While they probably killed the occasional mammoth or mastodon, it is unlikely that they built their lives around such large prey, which was already on the way to extinction and for which the area provided only a marginal habitat. Instead, small game, fish, and wild plants probably provided a large portion of their diet.

About 8000 B.C.E., global warming began to alter the environment dramatically. Sea levels rose to create the shoreline we know today. Huge volumes of glacial runoff flowed through the Allegheny, Susquehanna, and Delaware watersheds, raising the latter two rivers thirty feet above their current levels. When the waters abated, they left behind broad, flat, fertile stream terraces and countless small islands as ideal spots for human settlement. As the rivers assumed modern form, they also created other important structural characteristics. The Delaware, with its major tributaries the Lehigh and Schuylkill, and the Susquehanna with its North and West branches and its Juniata tributary, each partially traversed the natural barrier of the Appalachians to link the Delaware and Chesapeake bays with today's upstate New York. In the region defined by these two river systems, then, the enduring course of human interaction and development would flow roughly from south to north and back again. By contrast, the southward-flowing Allegheny and its tributaries joined the northward-flowing Monongahela system to form the Ohio, with its broad route westward toward the Mississippi. Here, therefore, the principal natural orientation was to the south and west, rather than the east, from which the region remained relatively inaccessible. While paths from the headwaters of the West Branch and especially the Juniata provided some access across the Plateau to the tributaries of the Allegheny, for the most part the westward-oriented Ohio watershed remained formidably isolated from the southward-flowing Susquehanna and Delaware systems.

Or, rather, it was the Susquehanna and Delaware watersheds that were isolated. For centuries, the centers of Native American population and cultural innovation in eastern North America lay in the Ohio and Mississippi valleys and, far to the southwest, among the great civilizations of Central America. The Susquehanna and Delaware watersheds could communicate with the core only indirectly by way of the coastal plains of the Great Lakes in the north and the Atlantic seaboard in the south. Far from being the keystone, Pennsylvania was on the very edge of the Native American world.

*   *   *

As the land of what became Pennsylvania assumed its three-part form, its plant and animal population changed. Over the course of many centuries, a succession of forests spread northward—first pine and spruce, then hemlock, and, by about 3000 B.C.E., oak and hickory. In the woods, acorns, hickory nuts, and undergrowth provided food for both people and the deer and small game they hunted. Far more abundant in resources were the waterways, which became major corridors for migrating ducks, geese, and other waterfowl. Teeming with freshwater fish throughout the ice-free months of the year, the

The Region's Ancient Past

Approximate Dates	Major Environmental Events	Cultural Change in the Region that became Pennsylvania
30,000-22,000 B.C.E.	Interior continental route from Beringia south ice-free	First migrations from Asia to the Americas
22,000-15,000 B.C.E.	Pacific coastal route south ice-free, interior route blocked	Migrations probably continue, South America occupied
15,000 B.C.E..	Glaciers begin to melt; Beringia submerged	Earliest occupation of Pennsylvania?
10,600 B.C.E..	Glaciers recede from today's Pennsylvania	Paleo-Indian Period
9500 B.C.E.	Younger Dryas cooling halts glacial melting	Paleo-Indian Period
8000 B.C.E.	Warming resumes; rivers and coastlines of Pennsylvania region begin to take modern form	Early Archaic Period
6500 B.C.E.	Oak forests predominate	Middle Archaic Period
3000 B.C.E.	Mixed oak and hickory forests	Late Archaic Period
1000 B.C.E.		Early Woodland Period
0 C.E.		Middle Woodland Period
900 C.E	Medieval Optimum period of global warming begins	Agricultural Revolution; Late Woodland Period
1350 C.E	"Little Ice Age" begins	Late Woodland Period
1500-1600 C.E		First contacts with Europeans
1624-1638 C.E		Dutch, Swedish, and English colonies established

Delaware and Susquehanna were invaded each spring by huge schools of salt-water herring, shad, and other species headed for spawning sites upstream.

The geographic and ecological transformation of Pennsylvania inspired the new cultural patterns of what is known as the Archaic Period, generally dated from about 8000 to 1000 B.C.E.. Gradually over the centuries, people populated the extended watersheds of each of the state's three major river systems and exploited the riches of the natural environment in sophisticated ways. Most evident in the archaeological record is a vast array of stone weapons and tools. Indeed, the majority of archaeological relics now resting in backyard gardens, attic cigar boxes, and amateur collections throughout Pennsylvania date from this era. The ubiquity of such artifacts suggests both the successful adaptation of human societies to every habitable portion of the landscape and the seasonal mobility that allowed relatively small populations to leave their marks nearly everywhere.

The proliferation of artifacts also reflects real technological innovations. Many were made with a time-consuming "ground-stone" technique, which used water and grit to shape and polish rocks. Axes, adzes, and other wood-working tools made by this method were very common, suggesting that people were making dugout canoes, clearing trees, and cutting firewood on a scale not previously seen. Ground-stone pestles, mortars, and similar devices for processing nuts and other food, along with bowls and cooking pots made of soft soapstone, meanwhile, indicate the use of a wide variety of food resources. So too do ground-stone fishnet anchors, platform hearths presumably used to dry the resulting catch, and carefully dug pits to store the produce.

Ground-stone axes and fishing-net sinkers. Painstakingly shaped and polished with water and grit, these items provide evidence of complex patterns of life in the Archaic Period, 8000-1000 B.C.E. *The Pennsylvania Historical and Museum Commission, Harrisburg.*

Such evidence indicates that, gradually through the Archaic Period, people began to spend more of the year in a single location. Local bands probably consisted of twenty-five to fifty individuals who hunted and gathered in a circumscribed area—most likely a stream drainage—of perhaps 500 square miles. A gendered division of labor almost certainly prevailed, in which women were primarily responsible for gathering, and men for hunting and fishing. Both activities required deep understanding of the landscape and its bounty. Gathering was hardly the random kind of activity its name might seem to imply. Women needed an encyclopedic knowledge of wild plants, for, in some seasons, the fruits and vegetables they harvested may have constituted the bulk of the band's diet. Hunters, meanwhile, intensely studied habits of the same kinds of game animals found in Pennsylvania's forests today. Deer, elk, bear, and turkey were significant food sources, but fish, shellfish, and fowl were probably just as important.

*   *   *

To the south and west of the three river systems that would define Pennsylvania, the Early Woodland Period that followed the Archaic beginning in approximately 1000 B.C.E., and the Middle Woodland Period that followed from about 0 to 1000 C.E., saw dramatic developments. In the Ohio Valley, the great civilizations known as Adena (Early Woodland) and Hopewell (Middle Woodland) developed rich material cultures, built huge earthworks at their ceremonial centers, and, through vast trading networks, spread their influence across much of the continent. Yet, because of their geographic isolation, the Allegheny and especially the Susquehanna and Delaware watersheds remained on the fringes of these influences. For the most part, people continued living much as their predecessors had done.

Two innovations deserve attention, however. Everywhere in eastern North America, the characteristic that distinguishes Early Woodland from Archaic archaeological sites is the presence of ceramic pottery. Either by coiling long filaments of clay or by shaping a single lump of material, potters—probably women—fashioned rough round-bottomed shapes and then used their hands and wooden paddles wrapped with cord to perfect the vessel's final appearance. By 800 B.C.E., virtually everywhere in the three watersheds, this general style of pot-making was evolving into distinct local variations—in the kinds of shell, rock, or grit mixed into the clay, in the particular decorative patterns etched into a pot's surface, and in the forms a collar did or did not elaborate around its mouth. The variations are so distinct for time and place that pottery styles must have carried great significance as symbols of group identity. Much like language and ceremonies, ceramic traditions helped define the cultural boundaries of a community.

By the first century C.E., the size of the largest ceramic vessels and village storage pits tended to increase. This phenomenon probably reflects the second important development of the era, the addition of cultivated plants to the wild vegetation that had long been a major part of Native diets. The change appears to have come gradually—the line between carefully tended natural vegetation and deliberately cultivated new varieties is not as clear as one might think—and basic ideas and seeds probably filtered into Pennsylvania from the centers of Adena and Hopewell innovation. The cultivators almost certainly were women, who as the principal gatherers had the necessary expertise with plants to experiment with new crops.

Although it is difficult to find conclusive archaeological evidence, in the Susquehanna and Delaware River watersheds wild rice and grasses such as goosefoot and pigweed probably grew wherever soils and other conditions permitted. The seeds of those plants joined hickory nuts, acorns, and butternuts, along with various roots, as foods ground into flours and eaten in soups and perhaps as bread. Sunflowers, widely cultivated in the Ohio Valley, probably also joined the list. Squashes and pumpkins—among the earliest domesticated plants throughout much of the Americas and grown in today's Illinois by 5000 B.C.E. and Kentucky by 2300 B.C.E.—have not been verified for the Susquehanna and Delaware watersheds in this period. Neither has maize, which, while common, was not yet planted on a large scale anywhere in eastern North America. In all three regions that would become Pennsylvania, if these crops were cultivated at all, they apparently played a minor role. Native

Such artifacts as this straight-sided earthenware pot, patterned after earlier vessels made of stone, and this Early Woodland conical ceramic pot—used for cooking and storage—allow us to glimpse ways of life 2,000 years ago, when formerly nomadic people adopted more settled living patterns. *The Pennsylvania Historical and Museum Commission, Harrisburg,* and Randall M. Miller and William Pencak, eds., *Pennsylvania: A History of the Commonwealth* (University Park: The Pennsylvania State University Press, 2002), p. 16. *Copyright 2002 by the Pennsylvania State University. Reproduced by permission of the publisher.*

women might better be described as gardeners than as farmers, and the gathering of wild plants remained their principal contribution to their bands' sustenance.

*   *   *

Two things stand out from this brief survey of what archaeologists have pieced together about the human history in what became Pennsylvania. First is the vast time scale: for over 10,000 years, the people and the landscape grew up together. This, as much as Europe or Africa, was an "old world." Just as striking is how slowly basic ways of life seem to have changed. Relatively few specific locales, inhabited repeatedly across the centuries, provided good sites for human subsistence, and technologies for exploiting them evolved slowly. The richest environments were in river valleys, where floodplains provided fertile soils for wild plants, where wetlands attracted small game, where migrating fish could be captured on their spawning runs, and where forest edges offered plant fibers, trees small enough to be cut with stone tools, and an array of vegetable foods. These forest edges were probably managed by periodic fires, set to encourage new floor growth that would attract deer and small game under the canopy of undamaged larger trees. The courses of streams, too, were modified by people's fish-trapping weirs. There was nothing "simple" or "primitive" about such practices, and for the most part life was anything but nasty, brutish, and short. Well-adapted material patterns thus endured, although an infinite variety of human languages, beliefs, and social practices—which leave hardly a trace in the archaeological record—no doubt came and went with the centuries.

Chapter 2

Agricultural Revolution, 1000-1500

In the years around 1000 C.E., the basic patterns of life that had prevailed for millennia began to change dramatically. A global warming trend known as the Medieval Optimum—an increase of a few degrees in average annual temperature that began in about 900 C.E. and lasted until the mid-1300s—fostered a great outburst of agricultural creativity that for the first time allowed people of the Pennsylvania region to rely on cultivated plants for a major portion of their diets. In variations that played out somewhat differently in each of the region's three river systems, this agricultural revolution produced new forms from ancient cultural materials.

*   *   *

Beans—grown in Central America for thousands of years and in southwestern North America for centuries but apparently not successfully adapted to the eastern North American environment until the onset of the Medieval Optimum—were central to the agricultural revolution. Only when legumes joined the diet could people successfully rely on corn as their staff of life, for corn's nutritional value on its own is very low. Beans and corn consumed together, however, provide a protein-rich diet. And, at the same time farmers were adapting beans, they were also improving strains of maize, particularly a variety known as Northern Flint. With a 90-day growing period, it was ideally suited to the vast stretches of eastern North America where the annual number of frost-free days averaged about 120. (The margin of error allowed for the inevitable spring and fall cold snaps.) In the transitional period when the new breed was evolving, the extended growing seasons of the Medieval Optimum would have made it particularly successful.

Everywhere the new agriculture spread in eastern North America, corn and beans travelled together with squash. The three usually grew not only in the same fields but symbiotically in the same hills. Corn stalks provided a natural pole around which growing bean vines could twine, while the beans, as nitrogen-fixing legumes, replenished modest amounts of a crucial element that corn tended to deplete from the soil. Meanwhile, squashes or pumpkins spread their broad-leaved vines to crowd out weeds and shade the

Native American women grinding corn. From François Du Creux, *Historiae Canadensis, sue Nouae-Franciae libri decem, ad annum usque Christi* (Paris, 1664). *Annenberg Rare Book and Manuscript Library, Van Pelt-Dietrich Library Center, University of Pennsylvania, Philadelphia.*

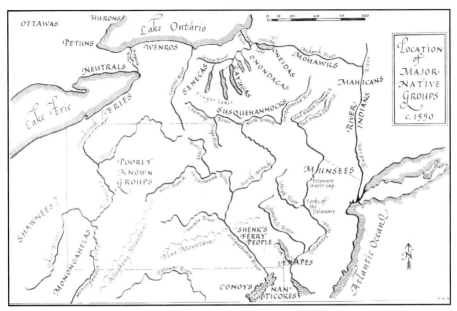

Map prepared by Kimberly Nichols.

ground, thus retarding evaporation under the hot sun. Together, the corn, beans, and squash thrived within an agricultural process of impressive simplicity. In easily worked floodplain soils, a digging stick to make a hole in which to plant the seeds and a hoe to build a hill around the growing plants were the only tools necessary. Once the squash vines began to spread, little weeding or other tending was necessary until the crops matured. The "Three Sisters" of corn, beans, and squash reinforced each other both in the field and in the cooking pot, where they provided a nutritiously abundant diet.

Initially, the new crops may simply have joined the repertoire of gathered vegetable foods women had long contributed to their families' diet. But over time, in many places in eastern North America, the Three Sisters became staples that contributed 50 to 75 percent of a community's food. Such heavy reliance on agriculture not only encouraged population to expand and villages to become firmly rooted in a single spot, but also allowed the women who grew the crops to exert significant economic and social power. That power substantially derived from the ecological setting in which the new agriculture emerged. North America lacked any species that could be domesticated as a source of animal protein. Hunting and fishing necessarily remained important economic activities. While women became increasingly sedentary to tend their crops, men continued ancient patterns of seasonal travels in pursuit of game and migratory fish and fowl. For the long portions of the year during which many men were away, agricultural villages became a largely female domain.

South and west of the Pennsylvania region, the agricultural revolution produced heights of productivity and supported population densities hitherto unimagined. After 900 C.E., a great new agricultural civilization (or, rather, cluster of civilizations) that scholars label "Mississippian" flourished there. Difficult routes of communication, however, ensured that innovations spread to the three river systems of Pennsylvania more slowly and less dramatically. Moreover, with the major exception of the main rivers and a few of their principal tributaries, the countless tiny streams that wind through the region's landscapes provided few of the floodplains best suited for cultivation. And today—although perhaps not during the Medieval Optimum—in many parts of the Allegheny watershed in particular, the average number of frost-free days dips below the minimum required for maize. Only limited areas of what became Pennsylvania were suited to the new agriculture, and in many of those, the conditions were marginal.

*   *   *

One such area stretched from present-day Pittsburgh south and west into nearby West Virginia and Ohio. There, from about 900 C.E. onward, people who shared a complex of archaeological traits called "Monongahela" made the best of their region's environmental limitations and came to rely on agriculture for roughly half of their diet. They lived in villages of perhaps three hundred people, usually in upland locations astride local watersheds draining in two directions, which allowed gatherers, fishers, and hunters to complement agriculture with wild plants, freshwater mussels, and game animals, especially white-tailed deer. Whether larger towns exploited the more favorable riverine locations now occupied by Pittsburgh and the Mon Valley steel mill sites may never be known, because urban and industrial development has destroyed so much archaeological evidence. Wherever they were located, Monongahela villages tended to be enclosed in a wooden palisade, with one or sometimes two rings of houses arranged around an open central plaza. Houses were circular, often with a distinctive half-buried storage room extending from one side. Whether the Monongahelas constituted a unified political entity, whether they all spoke the same language, and what relationship they had to later tribal groups, are mysteries.

The fertile plains along the Great Lakes coast and the valleys of the Finger Lakes and Mohawk Valley in present-day New York provided a more hospitable environment for the new agriculture. In this region, people associated with a complex of archaeological traits called "Point Peninsula" had long lived by the same kind of intensive gathering, fishing, and hunting supplemented by gardening that characterized other people of the region. After 900

C.E., however, villages in the area became larger and clearly based on agriculture, while Point Peninsula artifacts rapidly yielded to those known as "Owasco." The people who made these Owasco materials are among the few from this period who can be unequivocally identified as direct predecessors of the Native people who would interact with the European colonizers of Pennsylvania. They were the common ancestors of the Iroquois Five Nations or Haudenosaunee (Mohawks, Oneidas, Onondagas, Cayugas, and Senecas), the Susquehannocks, the Eries, and others who spoke languages of the Iroquoian family.

Owasco communities seem to have been extremely independent, isolated, and hostile toward outsiders. Gradually across the upper Susquehanna watershed and a sweep of territory from today's northwestern Pennsylvania through upstate New York, southern Ontario, and the St. Lawrence River valley, smaller communities consolidated into larger entities, and large villages into tribal groupings and confederacies. By the sixteenth century, at least two such alliances had been established. One formed in Ontario among the several Huron nations, and the other in central New York among the Five Nations of the Iroquois League. Around the margins of the Huron and Iroquois countries, other descendants of the Owasco peoples consolidated locally into substantial villages and perhaps confederacies, but remained aloof from the two leagues. Among these were at least two peoples of what Europeans would later call Pennsylvania. In villages scattered along the North Branch of the Susquehanna, and perhaps in a few outposts on the West Branch as well, lived the Susquehannocks, known to people of the Iroquois Five Nations as *Gandastogué*, the term that comes down to us as "Conestoga." The territory of the group known as Eries, meanwhile, included the extreme northwestern portion of today's Pennsylvania along the shores of the lake that now bears their name.

At its peak, the total Iroquoian-speaking population of the region that stretched from the upper Susquehanna watershed through much of today's upstate New York may have approached 100,000. An Iroquoian town could be home to as few as 300 or as many as 2,000 people. Packed within a perimeter of earthworks and wooden palisades enclosing up to sixteen acres were 30 to 150 buildings, the majority of which were distinctive structures called longhouses. Arranged side-by-side in parallel rows, they were usually about 20 feet wide and varied in length from 40 to 200 feet. Saplings twisted into the ground at close intervals provided the basic framework for exterior walls and an arched roof. Large sheets of elm bark secured by tree fibers enclosed the framework's sides and most of the rafters, while movable panels covered doorways at each end and rooftop openings that let smoke out and daylight in. Fireplaces were arranged at roughly 20-foot intervals along a central corridor

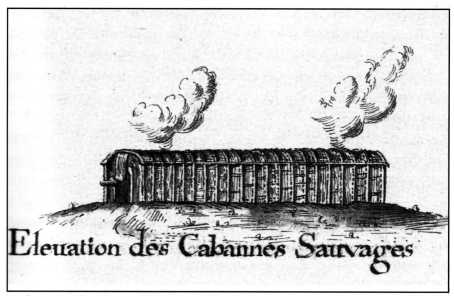

An Iroquoian longhouse. Detail from *Plan du Fort Frontenac our Cataraouy*, c.1720. *The Newberry Library, Chicago.*

and were flanked by raised platforms divided into compartments, each of which housed a nuclear family. The fireplaces, and thus heating and cooking facilities, were shared by two families occupying apartments on opposite sides of the house. All of the families in a longhouse were members of a single lineage traced through the female line—a group of elderly sisters, their daughters, and their grandchildren. Most often, but probably not always, men went to live with their wives' families after marriage. Hereditary titles of male authority also descended in the female line, from uncle to nephew, rather than from father to son. More generally within the longhouse, uncles—mothers' brothers—were the principal male role models and disciplinarians for children. Biological fathers, meanwhile, assumed a close but non-authoritarian role similar to that sometimes played by uncles in patrilineal societies such as those of Western Europe.

*   *   *

The agricultural revolution played out in yet a third way in the Delaware watershed. Just as clearly as the Owasco people were progenitors of the Iroquoians, the Late Woodland residents of the lower Delaware Valley were ancestors of those later known as Lenapes, which roughly translates from their Unami language as "original people." Remarkably little archaeological evidence has been found on pre-sixteenth-century inhabitants of the lower

Fanciful depiction of seventeenth-century Lenape people, based on a description given to a Swedish artist who had never been to North America. Detail of Pehr Lindestrom map, 1633, from Thomas Campanius Holm, *Kort beskrifning om Provincien Nya Swerige uti America* (Stockholm, 1702). *The Library Company of Philadelphia.*

Delaware River watershed, and almost nothing indicating long-term settlement, agriculture, or food storage has been discovered. How this lack of evidence should be interpreted is controversial. To some degree, it is explained by the fact that the now heavily urbanized belt from Wilmington to Trenton was surely the center of Lenape country, and its archaeological record has been almost thoroughly obliterated. The sandy, agriculturally marginal, coastal plain soils also would tend to minimize reliance on domesticated crops. As a result, some archaeologists conclude that the immediate ancestors of the Lenapes grew no corn at all but instead were gatherers and fishers who lived in small, mobile bands that left little mark on the landscape. Others argue, on the basis of documented evidence from later periods and comparisons with Algonquian-speaking peoples to the north and south along the Atlantic coast, that the Lenapes camped and fished in the woods during the winter, relocating to clearings and watersides in the spring, where they planted the Three Sisters and gathered wild plants.

North of the Unami-speaking Lenapes, beyond the Delaware Water Gap, lived people who spoke dialects of the closely related Munsee language. The poor soils of much of this region, scoured by glaciers that left little behind but rocks and gravel, make some scholars argue that gathering, fishing, and hunting continued to be the basis of Munsee subsistence long after the onset of the agricultural revolution elsewhere. Others stress contrary evidence, and in particular the patches of excellent soils that scatter the region. It should also be noted that Munsee-speakers exchanged agricultural products as well as furs with Henry Hudson's crew near Manhattan in 1609. One of Hudson's officers said the Natives had "great store of maize, or Indian wheat," from which they baked "good Bread."[3]

Despite the contradictory evidence, it seems clear that both upper and lower Delaware watersheds were home to numerous bands of a few dozen to a few hundred people who had participated less thoroughly in the agricultural revolution than peoples in the other regions of what later became Pennsylvania. These many small communities were for the most part autonomous, but they were united into loose regional political groupings that might best be described not as unified tribes but as collections of peoples who shared strong affinities of marriage, trade, and language with each other. As among their Iroquoian neighbors, kinship was primarily matrilineal. "The children of him that is now king, will not succeed, but his brother by the mother, or the children of his sister, whose sons (and after them the children of her daughters) will reign," William Penn explained a century later."[4] There were many such local "kings," however. This extreme localism may account for the somewhat redundant term *Lenni-Lenape*—"the real original people," which perhaps was used to distinguish one's own village from others nearby.

*   *   *

By the year Europeans reckoned as 1500, then, a dynamic period of historical change had created a landscape in which each of the three river systems was dominated by a different cluster of Native groups, each of which had worked out its own variation of the agricultural revolution: Monongahelas in the southwest, Iroquoian-speakers in the north and center, and Lenapes and Munsees in the east. Across the local variations and differences in language, culture, and beliefs, some common patterns prevailed. Everywhere, agricultural towns were, to a significant degree, female worlds. The gendered division of labor and the continued importance of hunting and fishing ensured that, for much of the year, villages would be inhabited primarily by women and their children, who tended the fields while males, accompanied by a few women and older children, dispersed to far-flung fowling locations in the spring and to hunting and trapping grounds in the fall and early winter. In the spring and early summer, older men travelled to fishing camps a day or more distant from the village. From spring through fall, warfare also drew young men away to make raids on often distant enemies. Only in mid- to late winter were most villagers of both sexes at home simultaneously for extended periods.

If a village's inhabitants changed over time, so too did its location. Despite the efficiency of women's agricultural practices, soil gradually lost

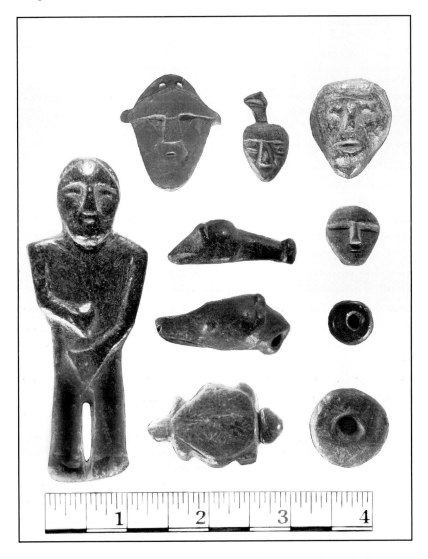

Stone effigies and coal beads from Iroquoian archaeological sites. *The Pennsylvania Historical and Museum Commission, Harrisburg.*

its productivity, and new fields ever farther from the main town had to be cleared of trees. Meantime, hundreds of people dependent on wood, bark, and vegetable fibers to make everything from houses to baskets created a voracious appetite for trees. Together the two trends gradually depleted the best parts of nearby forests. Within the village palisades, wood and bark construction materials steadily rotted, while longhouses and storage pits became infested with insects and other pests. After about two decades, a town site thus outlived its usefulness, and a community had to move on to start over in a different locale, usually a few miles away. At any given time, therefore, people needed not only the space occupied by their current town and its surrounding farmland, but also a spot for a new village under construction, sites for future towns, places where former settlements were undergoing a natural process of reclamation, a variety of fishing and fowling camps, and various hunting territories. What would look to later European colonists like empty countryside punctuated by widely scattered villages was, in fact, an actively used and essential landscape. Native people required extensive homelands to support their way of life.

That landscape, and nearly everything in it, was considered to be alive with an animating spiritual power. Such "other-than-human persons" as plants, game animals, trees, or the wind could either help people or bring them harm. The "Three Sisters" of corn, beans, and squash might agree to sustain everyone's life. Animals might choose to give themselves as food. Winds might restrain themselves to allow a canoe to cross a lake. In return, however, all of these spiritual beings demanded respect through the performance of ceremonies, the giving of thanks, the offering of sacred tobacco. If humans offended these beings by neglecting their reciprocal obligations, hunger, sickness, injury, or death could result. The basic idea was not so much that spirit-beings were inherently good or evil, but that the universe was full of forces of unequal power. Some were human, most other-than-human, but all had the potential either to be allies or enemies. To negotiate this complicated maze, humans had to make alliances—particularly with beings more powerful than themselves. These reciprocal, if asymmetrical, relationships and their ceremonial maintenance, rather than any specific set of dogmas, doctrines, or beliefs about the characteristics of particular spirits, were at the heart of religious experience.

In a more material realm, reciprocity similarly shaped ideas about property rights, which rested on need and use rather than mere possession and demanded that in the long run those who gave would also receive. Food, clothing, tools, houses, and land belonged to those individuals or kin groups who needed and made active use of them. Conversely, excess or abandoned property was largely free for the taking, and, in times of shortage, whatever was available was supposed to be shared by all. This communal ethic encouraged people not so much to accumulate goods but to be in a position to provide them to others. Social status and political authority went not to those who merely *had* the most, but to those who were in a position to *give* the most away. Far from ensuring a utopia of egalitarian bliss, the system encouraged rivalries for influence, yet channeled those rivalries into benefits for kin groups and the community as a whole. In this context, economic exchanges generally took the form of gift-giving rather than buying and selling. Exchanges of goods sealed relationships. If the gifts included rare items charged with spiritual significance—shells, exotic minerals, and other items associated with powerful beings who lived underwater or beneath the ground—the relationships could be powerfully extended into the supernatural world.

*   *   *

Among the Native peoples of the region, then, competition for authority as well as its exercise rested on the effectiveness with which people could build bonds of reciprocal obligation, and trade—both local and long-distance— took on political and even religious significance. Both patterns were deeply rooted in both the ancient past and the recent agricultural revolution. Both, too, would powerfully shape the responses of Native people to the arrival of people and things from new worlds across the sea.

Chapter 3

Discovering Europeans, 1500-1682

It is unclear when Native people of the Pennsylvania region first laid eyes upon Europeans. Some people who may have been Munsee residents of the Delaware Valley observed Giovanni da Verrazzano during his reconnaissance of New York Bay for the French crown in 1524. A party of Susquehannocks met John Smith when he sailed from Jamestown to the head of Chesapeake Bay in 1608. In the long interval between, surely rumors and stories of strangers arriving by water made their way to Native communities everywhere. And, just as the vast majority of Spaniards did not have to travel with Columbus to feel the effects of his voyages, Native people did not need to see an English face to feel the transformative impacts of contact with a world new to them. The ways in which Lenapes and Munsees, Susquehannocks and Monongahelas, responded to those impacts grew from their own historical traditions and from the cultural patterns developed in the agricultural revolution of recent centuries. This was an age of discovery for all peoples, but, for decades, most Indians of what would later be called Pennsylvania lived their lives out of sight of—and independent of—the European newcomers whose presence nonetheless had a growing impact on their societies.

* * *

Viruses from Europe may well have been the first living things to arrive in Native villages from across the Atlantic. The long isolation of North and South America from Europe, Africa, and Asia and their human, animal, and microbial populations made Indian peoples "virgin soil" for such common Eurasian and African illnesses as smallpox, measles, and influenza. There is not enough evidence to reach any firm conclusions about when people in the mid-Atlantic region first died from imported maladies. But it is reasonable to speculate that diseases erupted first in the lower Delaware and Susquehanna regions, where Indian travelers from the coast could have spread microbes to people who had not yet directly dealt with Europeans. Farther inland, epidemics probably did not strike until the early 1630s, when smallpox swept New England, the Great Lakes, and probably the Allegheny-Monongahela region. From that time forward, disease was omnipresent in Indian life. Whenever the epidemics began, they wrought enormous devastation. Once viruses hit a given area, population typically declined by 80 to 95 percent over the course of a century before reaching a new plateau. Because European observers came to the interior of today's Pennsylvania so late in the process, the vast majority of the deaths went unrecorded in their documents, and most of the Native people who might have preserved oral memories of the carnage failed to survive. One of the few pieces of direct testimony comes from the 1650s, when a Dutch colonist heard Munsee-speaking people "affirm, that . . . before the small pox broke out amongst them, they were ten times as numerous as they now are."[5]

Under such appalling circumstances, Indian communities did not just dramatically shrink. They had to recombine, resettle, and recoalesce into new entities. A village that used to be home to 500 people of various ages

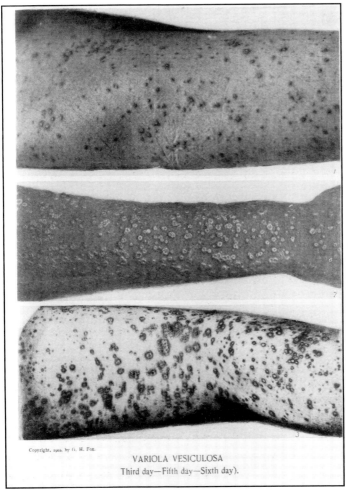

Copyright, 1902, by G. H. Fox.

VARIOLA VESICULOSA
Third day—Fifth day—Sixth day).

The horrific effects of smallpox, here illustrated at the third, fifth, and sixth days of an outbreak. From George Henry Fox, *A Practical Treatise on Smallpox* (Philadelphia, 1902). *The College of Physicians of Philadelphia.*

and abilities could not continue to function with 50 survivors skewed in their ages, sexes, and skills. Fragments had to join forces, and many formerly heavily populated areas became virtually empty. The people who survived to be known to European colonists as Lenapes, Munsees, or Susquehannocks were products of this ethnic mixing. Peoples such as the Monongahelas, who are identified only by the names later archaeologists gave them, lived on, if at all, only as submerged elements in other configurations.

*   *   *

The human landscape was also transformed by European material goods that found their way into Native communities before Indians ever laid eyes on a Dutch or English person. Passing from hand to hand through traditional forms of exchange, occasional items of European manufacture reached peoples of the Susquehanna region by 1550, having filtered northward from Natives who traded with or plundered Spanish and English ships on the shores of Chesapeake Bay and the Outer Banks of today's North Carolina. Somewhat later, the first European goods trickled into the Delaware Valley from various points along the Atlantic coast. Imports may not have arrived in the Monongahela area until nearly 1600, and then from the Potomac and Chesapeake, rather than from points directly east.

Rare things from across the ocean fit easily into ancient cultural patterns of ceremonial exchanges of exotic substances believed to embody spiritual power. The European items most likely to be unearthed from sixteenth-century archaeological sites in Pennsylvania are solitary glass beads and fragments of copper, brass, and iron, all of which corresponded in color, texture, and appearance to the sacred shells, chunks of minerals, and pieces of unsmelted copper that Indians had prized for centuries. People acquired and used these and other new goods as religious objects and sources of raw materials for Native-style tools, weapons, jewelry, and ritual items. A brass pot or an iron axe head was more likely to be cut up and reprocessed than to be employed as its European manufacturer intended. Before 1600 such items rarely, if ever, reached today's Pennsylvania intact in their original forms.

While the number of such goods was small, the items were evidently valuable enough to provoke violent struggles over access to them. Throughout northeastern North America, archaeological evidence shows that warfare intensified in the late sixteenth century. Struggles over access to valued items did not necessarily involve efforts to corner the market or to become commercial intermediaries between Europeans and rival Indian groups. Cultural patterns of reciprocity and redistribution probably led leaders (and would-be leaders) to acquire such goods in order to give them away to their followers, rather than to hoard them—at least until the items reached their final redistribution, when members of one clan ritually interred them in the grave of a deceased member of another kin group. If people were dying from strange diseases, this ritual motive for acquiring European goods may even have helped to intensify conflict over access to them. And because one of the ancient patterns of northeastern Indian warfare had been the adoption and incorporation of prisoners into the victors' communities, warfare in this period must also be placed in the context of killer epidemics. With people and their labor as perhaps the most valuable resource for disease-ravaged communities, the capture of prisoners was frequently more important than the effort to control trade routes or fur trapping territories.

Whatever the motives behind warfare, European goods became in their own right vital to military success, because improved weapons were

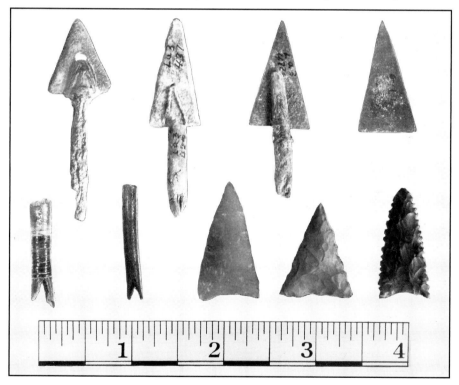

Brass objects made from pieces of trade kettles. Before about 1630, European metal was primarily used as raw material for Native-produced items. *The Pennsylvania Historical and Museum Commission, Harrisburg,* and Randall M. Miller and William Pencak, eds., *Pennsylvania: A History of the Commonwealth* (University Park: The Pennsylvania State University Press, 2002), p. 38. *Copyright 2002 by the Pennsylvania State University. Reproduced by permission of the publisher.*

among the most important things acquired by trade. Firearms entered the equation relatively late—probably in the 1630s in the Delaware and Susquehanna watersheds—and initially they were relatively insignificant. Early muskets were notoriously inaccurate, difficult to fire and maintain, and in many ways inferior to a skillfully aimed silent arrow. The more important innovations—indeed the object of a late sixteenth- and early seventeenth-century Native American arms race—were brass and iron arrowheads. These, like the other items fashioned by Indian craftspeople from the same scraps of kettles used to make jewelry and cutting tools, represented a vast improvement on the flint weapons that those without secure access to trade still had to use. Lighter and far sharper than their predecessors, they travelled farther and truer and could pierce the wooden body armor that had protected warriors from flint points. Meanwhile, sharp bits of copper or brass embedded in war clubs—and later entire hatchets made of iron—made unprecedentedly deadly weapons for hand-to-hand combat.

The experiences of the Susquehannocks illustrate the significance of early access to goods from Europe. The Susquehannocks' mid-sixteenth-century homeland in the upper Susquehanna left them less favorably situated than neighbors to the south, who were acquiring—probably from other Native people—small but significant quantities of glass beads and metal from the Chesapeake Bay region. At the same time, however, the Susquehannocks were more advantageously placed than their Onondaga Iroquois neighbors to the north, who had direct access neither to the Chesapeake nor to alternative sources on the Gulf of St. Lawrence. A complicated rivalry thus apparently pitted the Susquehannocks against their neighbors on all sides. Peoples from the Monongahela and Allegheny watersheds may also have been involved.

By the time European documents began to record events in the Susquehanna valley, the Susquehannocks had migrated southward to displace a culturally distinct "Shenks Ferry" population that formerly lived in what is today Lancaster County. Concentrated in a single large village near what is now Washington Boro, the Susquehannocks—still at war with their northern neighbors—enjoyed unimpeded access to sources of European goods on the Chesapeake Bay and probably reinforced their numbers with conquered remnants of the people they dispossessed.

*   *   *

The Susquehannock migration occurred at least a generation before any European outposts had been established in the neighborhood of Pennsylvania. Not until 1624 did the Dutch West India Company establish Fort Nassau on the Delaware River at today's Gloucester, New Jersey, and that post would be abandoned between 1627 and 1633. Meantime, in 1630, a Virginia English trader named William Claiborne purchased Kent Island in Chesapeake Bay from the Susquehannocks and began supplying them with imported goods in exchange for furs. In 1634 the arrival of colonists in Maryland (which claimed Kent Island but, because of the Susquehannocks' military might, could not eject the Virginian they protected) added additional sources of trade goods. Then, in 1638, the New Sweden Company established Fort Christina on the site of Wilmington, Delaware, a location easily reached from the Susquehannocks' country. So began a half-century of rivalry among various European competitors for the Pennsylvania region's Indian commerce, and of Indian rivalries for access to various trading centers and to sources of furs that could be used to purchase imported items. As the struggles intensified, a secure supply of European goods and weapons became vital to Indian survival in their struggles against Native foes.

When metal and other goods became more plentiful, the use of imports as raw material for Native crafts was joined by the wholesale substi-

Trade goods unearthed from Susquehannock archaeological sites include, clockwise from left, a rum bottle, beads, a spoon, a snuffbox, glass beads and a Swedish ceramic bowl, brass kettles, a flintlock musket mechanism, a metal harpoon, a cut Delft ceramic disk, brass arrowheads, iron axe heads, a jaw harp, and tobacco pipes. *The Pennsylvania Historical and Museum Commission, Harrisburg.*

tution of European goods for Native items: brass kettles for clay pots, woolen cloth for animal skins, glass beads for sea shells, firearms as frightful adjuncts to metal-tipped arrows. Still, the new items fit into traditional cultural niches and continued to be used in familiar ways, a fact to which European producers quickly adapted by designing varieties of cloth, tools, weapons, and jewelry specifically for Indian customers. The substitution of specially made European goods for domestically produced items did not necessarily mean the loss of Native craft traditions. While some skills declined—pot-making, for instance, virtually ceased when brass kettles became commonplace—others blossomed. Metal tools allowed both old and new materials to be worked in ways firmly rooted in Native traditions to produce stunning jewelry, combs, and other items. In some ways, the seventeenth century was a golden age of

Susquehannock hair combs carved from antler with imported iron tools show a degree of artistic detail unimaginable before the availability of European trade goods. *The Pennsylvania Historical and Museum Commission, Harrisburg*, and Randall M. Miller and William Pencak, eds., *Pennsylvania: A History of the Commonwealth* (University Park: The Pennsylvania State University Press, 2002), p. 40. Copyright 2002 by the Pennsylvania State University. *Reproduced by permission of the publisher.*

Native material culture. But it was also the age when people of the region became irrevocably dependent on trade with Europe.

Much of the new artistic energy went into artifacts associated with the spiritual realm: ritual masks, ceremonial pipes, and, most notably, a complex of activities associated with sacred wampum beads. Like other exotic substances, the shells of the whelk and the quahog clam—respectively white and "black" (actually purple) in color—were highly valued in much of eastern North America long before European contact. Seen by inland peoples in particular as gifts from an underwater realm of spirit-beings, the rare early beads came in many sizes and shapes. However, "true wampum"—small tubular beads finely drilled for stringing—became possible only with the introduction of iron tools. In the 1620s, as Dutch traders established their trading posts in the Hudson and Delaware valleys, they discovered a huge market for shell beads and introduced standardized techniques for wampum manufacture to

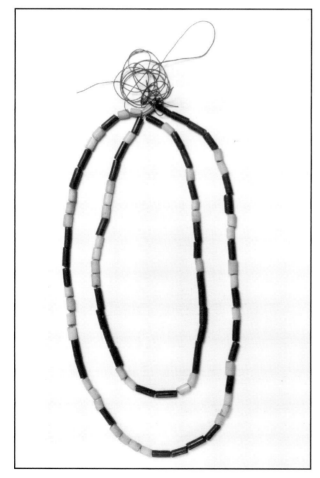

Strings of wampum.
Courtesy of the University of
Pennsylvania Museum
(Negative #70-9-304).

Algonquian peoples of the southern New England coast, where whelk and quahog were abundant. By the late 1630s, these Indians were churning out the tiny beads by the tens of thousands, to be traded for European manufactures from the Dutch, who would in turn exchange the wampum for furs from peoples farther in the interior. Iroquoians, in particular, quickly made wampum beads, strings, and belts integral to much of their religious and political life. But Lenapes and Munsees, too, invested the shell beads with enormous significance. "In case of any wrong or evil fact, be it murder itself," William Penn observed, "they atone by feasts and presents of their wampum, which is proportioned to the quality of the offence or person injured."[6]

With goods such as sacred wampum, newly indispensable tools, and coveted weapons at stake, in the mid-seventeenth century military conflicts spiralled out of control. For all the Natives involved, new weapons made warfare unprecedentedly deadly, and the devastation was compounded by continued outbreaks of imported diseases. The mid-century struggles did not so much produce winners as survivors. In this grim environment, the peoples most likely to survive were those with the strongest trading ties to Europeans: the Iroquois Five Nations, whose principal trading partners were the Dutch of Fort Orange (later Albany) on the Hudson River, and the Susquehannocks, who could choose on the Chesapeake between traders from Virginia or Maryland, and on the Delaware between the Dutch and the Swedes who, in the short independent lifetime of their colony before 1655, came to command the lion's share of their business.

*   *   *

In their supremely advantageous position, and with apparently firm control of hunting territories throughout much of the Susquehanna watershed, the Susquehannocks prospered for a generation. In about 1645, at the peak of their power, they relocated to a new, heavily fortified town a short distance south of their previous home. There between 3,000 and 5,000 people, many of them no doubt adopted war captives, lived in a flourishing economy increasingly dependent on trade for weapons, tools, cooking utensils, and countless other everyday goods. From the Susquehannock town, goods also moved northwestward through a trading network that included such Great Lakes Iroquoian people as the Eries and the Hurons.

Early Swedish and Dutch colonists, whose knowledge of the interior's geography and inhabitants was extremely sketchy, referred to all of the participants in this Susquehannock network as "Minquas," a Unami-derived word that roughly translates as "Iroquoian-speakers." Colonists sometimes further distinguished between "White Minquas"—by which they meant the

Susquehannocks themselves—and a more mysterious western group they called "Black Minquas," because they wore badges of that color. The presence of distinctive ornaments made of black coal on southwestern Pennsylvania archaeological sites suggests to some scholars that the Monongahelas may have been those people, but theories abound. The mystery results from the fact that, as communities largely cut off from direct sources of European trade but not from epidemic diseases, inlanders fared worst in warfare. Before the seventeenth century's midpoint, the Monongahelas, Eries, and perhaps other peoples of the western watersheds disappeared from the map, and most of the Allegheny, Monongahela, and upper Ohio region was entirely depopulated. The survivors were incorporated into the victorious villages of the Five Nations, and perhaps of the Susquehannocks as well.

Susquehannock military and economic dominance did not last long. War with their Native neighbors to the north and south was almost constant— Susquehannock defenders bloodily repulsed a massive Seneca Iroquois assault on their town in 1663, for instance—and epidemics, particularly smallpox in the early 1660s, struck several times. By about 1665, population was declining.

Fanciful depiction of a "Gyant like" Susquehannock man, demonstrates how little Europeans actually knew about the people who dominated the economic and military map of what became Pennsylvania in the mid-seventeenth century. Detail from John Smith, *A Map of Virginia* (Oxford, 1612). *Annenberg Rare Book and Manuscript Library, Van Pelt-Dietrich Library Center, University of Pennsylvania, Philadelphia.*

What, exactly, transpired next is unclear, but, within a decade, most surviving Susquehannocks would be forced to seek refuge, first in Maryland, and then with their erstwhile Iroquois Five Nations enemies. The majority were absorbed into Iroquois villages. Only a relative handful—among them the core of the group that later lived at Conestoga Manor—remained on the land their grandparents had conquered.

While all this was occurring in the interior, most Lenapes seem to have retreated from the west bank of the Delaware to locations in today's state of New Jersey; this may have been a result of a military defeat at the hands of the Susquehannocks in 1634, but the evidence is unclear. During this same period, the Lenapes apparently reached a diplomatic accommodation with the Iroquois Five Nations. According to traditions recounted several generations later, they renounced war and accepted a symbolic status as "women" charged with peacemaking among all the region's peoples. If the tradition is an accurate description of events (and some later Delaware leaders vigorously disputed it), the feminine title was rooted in the matrilineal social organization that Lenapes and Iroquois shared, in which clan mothers indeed controlled vital political decisions about war and peace. Whatever the Lenapes' diplomatic status among their Native neighbors, as the colonial population grew, they increasingly relied on the maize agriculture that may not previously have been of much importance to their livelihood—less to feed themselves than to acquire trade goods. Cut off from the prime sources of fur-bearing animals controlled by the Susquehannocks, they sold the colonists instead their crops, along with baskets and other craft items, and, ultimately, plots of their land.

*   *   *

In 1682, then, when William Penn first set foot in the colony King Charles II proclaimed to be his proprietary, he entered anything but a "virgin land." The Susquehanna and Monongahela-Allegheny-Ohio watersheds had been virtually emptied of settled inhabitants, although their ancient pathways and rivers continued to be used heavily by Indian traders and warriors from elsewhere. In the lower Delaware, meanwhile, the Lenape population had shrunk dramatically during two generations of direct experience with European colonists, with whom trade had become vital. As a result, when Lenapes met Penn face-to-face in 1682—when they enacted the reality enshrined mythically in West's and Hicks's paintings—they probably saw the event less as an historical turning point than as one more episode in a turbulent era. Swedes, Dutch, Finns, and other English, had, after all, come and gone for over fifty years. Why should these newcomers be any different?

Chapter 4
Uneasy Peace, 1682-1754

The seeming ordinariness of the encounter between Penn and the Lenapes reveals three factors that made the establishment of Pennsylvania distinctive in the history of English North American colonization. First, trade, rather than military conflict, had defined relationships between Indians and Europeans in the Delaware watershed already for decades before 1682. In part, this was because the European population was too small to represent much of a threat, but mostly it stemmed from a second factor. The real action, the real threat, was in the Susquehanna valley and points west, among Native people rather than between Indians and Europeans, who were generally welcomed for the weapons and other goods

Chalk portrait presumed to be of William Penn, by Francis Place, c. 1696. *The Historical Society of Pennsylvania.*

they could supply. Third, and just as important, on the eve of Penn's arrival, those military conflicts had imposed their deadly peace on the now virtually empty landscape of the Susquehanna and Monongahela-Allegheny-Ohio territories. These facts of Indian history help explain the long period of peaceful relations that ensued between Pennsylvania and its Native neighbors. Yet they also pointed to trouble in the future, as temporarily emptied lands began to fill again with contending groups of Native refugees and European colonists.

*   *   *

Just as important in explaining the long period of peace, and the underlying tensions it masked, are several distinctive aspects of the Pennsylvania colony and its government. Basic to the equation is the pacifism of William Penn and his fellow Quakers. Remarkably, for the better part of seventy years, the government had no military forces at its disposal, no infrastructure of militias, troops, warships, or artillery. As long as Quakers remained dominant in the colony, its relations with Native people inevitably had to rely on diplomacy rather than brute force.

Penn's Quaker values also led him to insist that all lands acquired for European settlement be purchased from the Native owners who were "true lords of the soil." Technically, then, when Penn wrote a letter from London to the Lenapes in 1681 announcing that "the king of the country where I live, hath given unto me a great province" he meant that his monarch had given him the sole right to purchase their lands from them. "Very sensible of the unkindness and injustice that hath been too much exercised towards you by the people of these parts of the world," Penn professed his "desire to win and gain your love and friendship, by a kind, just, and peaceable life" and announced that he had dispatched "commissioners to treat with you about land, and a firm league of peace."[8]

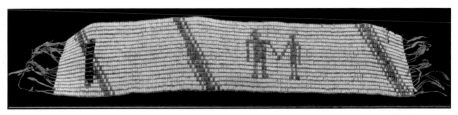

The Penn Treaty Wampum Belt, said to represent the agreement made between William Penn and the Lenapes in 1682, depicts a stout European with a broad Quaker hat clasping hands with a Native American. *Courtesy of the Historical Society of Pennsylvania Collection, Atwater Kent Museum of Philadelphia.*

The responsibilities of those commissioners—led by Penn's Deputy Governor William Markham—highlight another important element in the equation. Despite the sincerity of Penn's pacifism and his commitment to justice, the acquisition of Indian land was crucial to the success of Pennsylvania. Although the king's grant is often described as a reward for William Penn's father's loyal service to the Stuart family and as a settlement of a £16,000 royal debt to the family, the process of extracting a charter from the royal bureaucracy and launching the colony had cost Penn as much as £12,000. Recouping that cost and paying other debts that resulted from poor business decisions and legal problems were never far from his mind.

The delicate balance between Quaker religious experiment and worldly real estate venture held as long as William Penn himself remained in charge of his colony. By 1685, Penn and his agents had made at least eleven purchases from Lenape headmen, most of them vaguely defined by streams and other landmarks and several of them overlapping each other. Yet, by the early 1730s, this process had only managed to gain the Penn family uncontested title to about five percent of today's state, consisting of a rough triangle

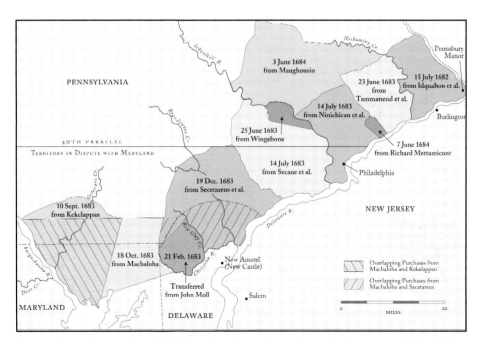

Approximate boundaries of William Penn's purchases from the Lenapes, 1682-1684. Map prepared by Adrienne Gruver, as revised with the assistance of Louis M. Waddell from Richard S. Dunn and Mary Maples Dunn, eds., *The Papers of William Penn* vol. 2 (Philadelphia, 1982).

between the Delaware and Susquehanna rivers below South Mountain and north of the fortieth parallel, below which Maryland would bitterly dispute Pennsylvania's claim until the 1760s, when Mason and Dixon surveyed their famous line at 39° 43'.

By that time, Penn himself was long gone from the scene. He left Pennsylvania for the last time in 1701, suffered a severe stroke in 1712, and then remained in very poor health until his death in 1718. In this period, he exercised little influence over what transpired in his province, as first his second wife Hannah and then his sons John, Thomas, and Richard—none of whom, as converts to Anglicanism, shared their parents' commitment to Quaker values—struggled both to pay the family's huge debts and counter challenges to their authority from the son of Penn and his first wife. As the family deficit continued to mount, the younger Penns began making major speculative land grants in hopes of recovering some of their financial losses from quitrents, annual fees due (but seldom actually paid) from property holders to the proprietor. Meantime, they deeded additional thousands of acres to themselves as private persons, from which they hoped to profit more directly. Much of the territory had not yet been purchased from its Indian owners, and no profits could be realized until it was.

Quite apart from the desperate financial straits of Penn's sons (in 1734 John actually had to flee England to avoid imprisonment for debt), several factors made acquiring title to large Indian tracts ever more pressing. One derived from a fundamental cultural conflict over the nature of rights to what the English called "real estate." Lenapes—like all Native people in eastern North America—conceived of property rights more in terms of use than of possession. In their earliest transactions with Swedes, Dutch, and English, and perhaps even in their first treaties with Penn himself, Lenape leaders almost certainly thought they were merely granting colonists temporary privileges to use land for crops, houses, and other purposes, rather than permanently transferring what Europeans, with their very different views of property, called the "right of soil." The drastically reduced numbers of post-epidemic Lenapes had plenty of territory to spare and thus eagerly agreed to such grants, but had no reason to expect that they would have to leave their homes as a result, or that the privileges they granted would not have to be renewed through additional payments in subsequent years. Moreover, among the highly decentralized Lenapes—particularly as their population reshuffled in the wake of epidemics—spokesmen for multiple kin groups in various villages might well assert legitimate claims to payment for the right to use a particular patch of ground their ancestors had shared. The result was that colonists found themselves paying repeatedly for what they thought should be a clear-cut, one-time transaction.

In the early eighteenth century, misunderstanding shaded into deliberate manipulation by both sides. Treaties written in English that most
Lenapes could not read for themselves described boundaries with deliberate
ambiguity to allow the most capacious interpretation. Native leaders, meanwhile, repeatedly came forward to assert claims to lands the English thought
they had already purchased—perhaps because claims legitimately overlapped,
perhaps in a deliberate effort to play a game similar to that of the Europeans.
As a result, Penn's agents did all they could to extract ever more stringent evidence that deeds extinguished all possible claims, to the largest possible tracts,
once and for all. Many years later, a Delaware tradition metaphorically
recalled the schemes of this period:

> As the whites became daily more familiar with the
> Indians, they at last proposed to stay with them,
> and asked only for so much ground for a garden
> spot as, they said, the hide of a bullock would
> cover or encompass, which hide was spread
> before them. The Indians readily granted this
> apparently reasonable request; but the whites
> then took a knife, and beginning at one end of the
> hide, cut it up to a long rope, not thicker than a
> child's finger, so that by the time the whole was
> cut up, it made a great heap; they then took the
> rope at one end, and drew it gently along, careful-
> ly avoiding its breaking. It was drawn out into a
> circular form, and being closed at its ends,
> encompassed a large piece of ground.[9]

By the 1730s, the suspicions and confusions were infinitely compounded by the fact that Lenapes were no longer the only people involved. In
the past half-century, various groups had resettled much of the upper
Delaware, the Susquehanna, and the western watersheds now collectively
known as "the Ohio country." Most prominent among them were Shawnees,
an Algonquian-speaking people whose ancestral homes were probably in
today's state of Ohio but who had dispersed widely during the seventeenth-
century Indian wars. Also significant were bands of Munsees and Lenapes—
collectively coming to be known as "Delawares"—pushed out of lands in New
Jersey and either returning to ancestral territories on the upper Delaware or
finding new homes in the Susquehanna. These groups—their decentralized
political traditions accentuated by the stresses of migration—were joined by
an array of migrants from almost every point on the compass: Mahicans from
the Hudson River valley; Algonquian-speakers from southern New England;

Nanticokes, Conoys and others from the Chesapeake region; Tuscaroras from the Carolinas who fled northward to join the Iroquois League as its Sixth Nation beginning in the 1710s; families from other Iroquois nations who moved southward and westward. Some of these people were returning to lands on which their ancestors had lived; perhaps those ancestors had been war captives of the Iroquois or Susquehannocks. Other newcomers, defeated in conflicts with Euro-Americans or deprived of their homes by treaties they considered unjust, were seeking refuge wherever they could find it. Some settled in ethnically defined villages, others in mixed places that could only be described as "Indian." Few of them recognized any central authority, Native or European, and none were in the mood to sell their lands and move again—although many were quite willing to grant privileges to traders and individual European families who could profitably share the territory with them.

And those European families vastly complicated the situation for Pennsylvania authorities trying to assert legal title to lands occupied by diverse Indian peoples. In the years after William Penn's death, thousands of Scots-Irish and German immigrants streamed through the port of Philadelphia seeking freedom from religious persecution and economic privation in their homelands—this at the very moment that Penn's heirs' legal troubles had virtually closed the provincial land office and made it practically impossible to issue valid land titles to the newcomers. Even if the land office had been fully functioning, these two immigrant groups would have presented particular problems. The Scots-Irish, many of them fleeing rapacious English landlords in Ulster, were hardly eager to embrace the Penn family as their new masters. Many moved west into either proprietary or Indian lands with little regard to the niceties of land title and no intention of paying quitrents. Meanwhile, Germans were not legally entitled to own land in an English province at all without special dispensation from the legislature until Parliament's passage of a general naturalization act in 1740. Yet they, too, were taking up lands in their thousands in the 1720s and 1730s.

"As the numbers of these People encrease upon us, so will the Difficulties of settling them," Pennsylvanian James Logan understated in 1728.[10] As the proprietors' personal agent, as secretary of the province, and as commissioner of property for three decades after the founder's departure in 1701, Logan became the central figure in Pennsylvania's early eighteenth-century relations with Native people. A land speculator and fur trader in his own right, he had mixed his private interests with those of the Penn family to engage in vast real estate ventures, some of which involved territories not yet officially purchased from their Indian owners. So he had strong personal, as well as official, motives to solve the vexing problem of acquiring legal title before any more land was unofficially occupied by immigrants.

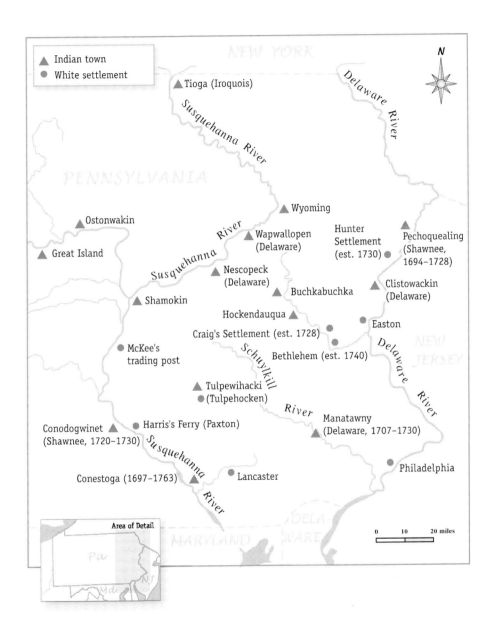

The Susquehanna and Delaware Valleys, 1700-1740. From *At the Crossroads: Indians and Empires on a Mid-Atlantic Frontier, 1700-1763* by Jane T. Merritt. Copyright © 2003 by the University of North Carolina Press. Used by permission of the publisher.

Compounding the problem, Logan repeatedly complained, were Maryland officials who tried to legitimate their claims to disputed territory by issuing titles to squatters and endorsing armed resistance against Pennsylvania authority. The contest with Maryland highlights the hard-headed, practical reason that Logan and the younger Penns had to follow at least the external forms of the founder's treaty policies. New York, Virginia, and even Connecticut—not to mention New France—also claimed Indian territories Pennsylvania considered within the bounds of its patent. In European courts, the colony that possessed clear Native title also possessed powerful ammunition in such controversies, so it was evermore vital that Pennsylvania establish a convincing paper trail.

Pennsylvania provincial secretary James Logan was a major architect of Pennsylvania Indian policy in the 1730s. Portrait by Thomas Sully (after Gustavus Hesselius), 1831. *The Library Company of Philadelphia.*

Yet who among the decentralized multiethnic Indian communities of the Delaware and Susquehanna watersheds could sign the necessary documents? Logan's brilliant solution was to identify a central authority that, in his and the Penns' minds, would speak for all the Indians concerned—whether those Indians recognized that authority or not. Factions within the Iroquois Six Nations had, for their own reasons, long been seeking a closer alliance with Pennsylvania as a counterbalance to the diplomatic, military, and economic vise in which their powerful neighbors in the colonies of New France and New York threatened to trap them. Their seventeenth-century wars against inhabitants of the Susquehanna and Ohio countries gave them pretense to a right of conquest over their lands, and Iroquois claims were bolstered by the assertion that many (although not all) of the Indian refugees who had resettled the territories did so at the Six Nations' invitation. Neither of these arguments, however, clearly applied to Munsee and Lenape territory. Neither people had ever been conquered, or even apparently engaged in significant warfare with, the Six Nations.

Nonetheless, Logan and the younger Penns overlooked such niceties and decided to go over the heads of the Lenapes to get the land cessions they needed from the Iroquois. As Logan put it in a letter to John Penn in 1731, if the province were to achieve its goals, "there will be an absolute necessity of treating with the Five Nations and securing their friendship more effectually."[11] Seeing in Pennsylvania the potential benefits of a powerful diplomatic protector and trading partner, leaders of the now Six Nations of the Haudenosaunee became willing partners. The key events in this Pennsylvania-Iroquois alliance were two treaties in 1736, one made publicly in a ceremonial visit of Six Nations headmen to Philadelphia and the other secured less decorously by Logan's agent Conrad Weiser at the Susquehanna Valley Indian town of Shamokin as the Iroquois delegation headed homeward. In the Philadelphia treaty, the Six Nations formally ceded all claims to lands on both sides of the Susquehanna River below North Mountain. By the second, secret, agreement, the Iroquois also "released[d] and quit all their claims" between the Delaware and Susquehanna Rivers south of the same highlands—territory to which the Six Nations had never made any pretense in the first place.[12] Although the Iroquois made this fact clear to Weiser at the time, Logan and the Penns translated this paper release of non-existent possession into a positive grant.

The lands in question included one particularly important tract, known to the Penns as "the Forks of the Delaware" and to the Lenapes as *Lechauwekink*, a word that colonists rendered as *Lehigh*. In recent decades, this area had become a main center for Lenapes who tried to remain within their ancient territory rather than migrate westward. Among these were a man from near Trenton, New Jersey, called Old Captain Harris and his son Teedyuscung. Unami was Teedyuscung's first language, but his training in Native traditions was spotty and he spoke English fairly well. In this, he was not at all atypical for Lenapes of his generation, who had always lived in close proximity to Euro-Americans. As a young adult on the fringes of colonial society, he sold baskets and brooms to support himself until the two men moved to the Forks in about 1730. Although the family had no hereditary claim to office, Teedyuscung's speaking talents allowed him to rise quickly to a prominent position. Yet everyone seemed to acknowledge that the legitimate leader at the Forks was a man named Nutimus, who probably was born there and apparently had a hereditary title.

As early as 1700, Nutimus announced his clear intention to defend the lands and the people gathering at the Forks from English expansion. In that year, William Penn agreed with a Lenape chief named Mechkilikishi upon terms for surveying lands that he had previously purchased south of the Forks. An elaborate plan called for two Europeans and two Indians to stroll along the banks of the Delaware River and its Tohickon Creek tributary as far as they could in a day and a half—while making sure to stop for a leisurely lunch during which their pack horse was to be unloaded and then reloaded. From the

stopping point, a line was to be drawn toward the setting sun to define the purchase boundary. Midway through the first afternoon of the walk, a dispute
arose when Penn's men insisted on crossing Tohickon Creek into territory over
which Nutimus claimed jurisdiction. He refused to let them pass, the survey
party broke up with its work uncompleted, and, for all intents and purposes,
Tohickon Creek—twenty miles or so south of the Forks—remained the northern boundary of Pennsylvania. This affair constituted the first, and by far least
controversial, "walking purchase" that affected the Lehigh Valley.

The second, and far more famous, of 1737, was made possible by the
1736 deal between Logan and the Iroquois. In 1732, Thomas Penn had
claimed to have discovered in the province's papers an early draft of the first
walking purchase treaty his father had made with Mechkilikishi in 1700—a
draft that omitted such important pieces of information as the date of the
agreement and the direction the survey walkers were to go. It may well have
been an outright forgery. Probably because Penn knew Nutimus could contra-
dict him if he dated the document to 1700, he claimed that it referred to a
land sale made between Lenapes and his father in 1686, long before Nutimus's
time. The proprietors' story, then, was that the second Walking Purchase was
not really a purchase at all, but instead merely the implementation of a half-
century-old agreement that now only needed to be reconfirmed by re-walking
the boundaries originally agreed upon. The Penns set scouting parties into the
woods literally to blaze a trail likely to take in the most territory in a thirty-six-
hour trek. Nutimus's repeated objections led to a blunt declaration in 1735
that the walk would take place whether he approved or not.

The 1736 agreements with the Iroquois gave the Penns the legal cover
they needed for their scheme and—more importantly—robbed Nutimus of
any political and diplomatic support he might have received from the Iroquois.
Under extreme pressure from both Pennsylvania and the Six Nations, and
undercut by such other Delaware chiefs as Lapowinsa and Tishcohan, who
had been courted (and had their portraits painted) by the government, the
Forks leader had almost no choice but to agree in August 1737 that the walk
could take place. But even that agreement could only be achieved through an
act of almost incredible Pennsylvania audacity. At a treaty council in
Philadelphia, Thomas Penn showed Nutimus and other Delaware headmen a
poorly drawn map that led them to believe they were agreeing to only a very
limited survey of lands along Tohickon Creek. English-language labels (which
may have been added after the council was over) identified the stream the
Indians thought was the Tohickon as the "West Branch River Delaware," or
what is today called the Lehigh.[13] When the walkers—or rather sprinters—
hired by the province to carry out the charade had completed their day-and-
a-half journey (variously estimated by scholars at between fifty-five and sixty-

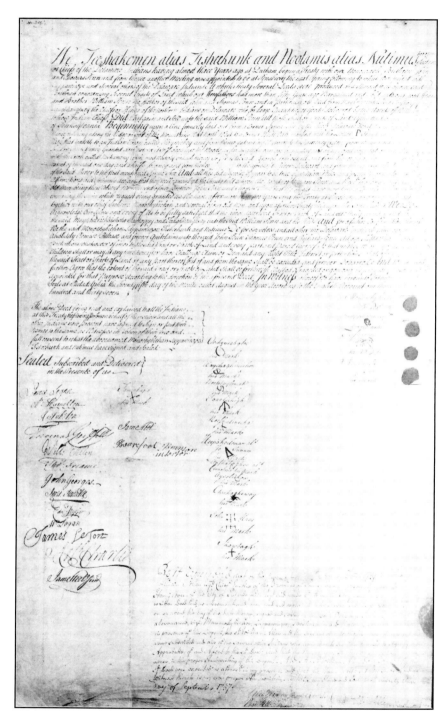

The "Walking Purchase" Treaty of 1737. RG-26, *Records of the Department of State, Pennsylvania State Archives, Harrisburg.*

five miles), they had enlarged the province by something on the order of twelve hundred square miles. The territory encompassed all of the lands on which Nutimus's people lived and the sites of today's cities of Bethlehem, Allentown, and Easton. Only about 6,500 acres around the village known as Nutimus's Town was set aside as a proprietary manor on which the Forks Indians could reside, at least temporarily. Euro-American settlers quickly moved into the Walking Purchase, taking up lands long since granted them by the Penn family. By 1740, more than one hundred families had taken up residence, despite the Forks Indians' strenuous protests. A year later, these were joined by the first of several German-speaking religious communities of the *Unitas Fratrum*, or Moravians, established at Bethlehem.

Lenape chiefs Lapowinsa (left) and Tishcohan (right), painted by Gustavus Hesselius, c. 1735. *Courtesy of the Historical Society of Pennsylvania Collection, Atwater Kent Museum of Philadelphia.*

Nutimus and the Forks Indians denied the right of any of these migrants to invade their lands, but the political forces arrayed against them became clear at a treaty council the Penns' lieutenant-governor George Thomas called at Philadelphia in 1742, a council at which Nutimus hoped for a fair hearing of his grievances. Thomas declared to the Six Nations delegations present that he expected them to "cause these Indians to remove from the Lands in the Forks of Delaware, and not give any further Disturbance to the Persons who are now in Possession." In response, the Onondaga orator Canasatego delivered a remarkable speech to the Lenapes:

> How came you to take upon you to sell land at all? We conquered you, we made women of you. You know you are women, and can no more sell land than women. . . . We charge you to remove instantly. We don't give you the liberty to think about it. . . . We, therefore, assign you two places to go—either to Wyoming [the modern Wilkes Barre area] or Shamokin. You may go to either of these places, and then we shall have you more under our eye, and shall see how you behave.[14]

This harangue—clearly designed more for Thomas's ears and Euro-American written documents than for Forks Indians—in several ways is as brazenly mendacious as the map deception perpetrated on Nutimus five years earlier. The Iroquois had never conquered the Lenapes. And, as previously mentioned, to the extent that the Lenapes had been characterized metaphorically as "women" (a characterization Teedyuscung, among others, denied), the term was probably one of respect, not derision, for their role as peacemakers. But most remarkable of all was Canasatego's claim that women had no right sell land. In his own Haudenosaunee tradition, women—the farmers who controlled a village's cornfields—were the only ones who *could* convey use rights to others. *Men* were the ones who had no right to sell land on their own.

                              *   *   *

Nonetheless, the message recorded in Euro-American documents was clear. Most of the Forks Lenapes had little choice but to move on. As Canasatego directed, many went to new homes at Shamokin or Wyoming, where Teedyuscung presided as "King of the Delawares" and repeatedly protested

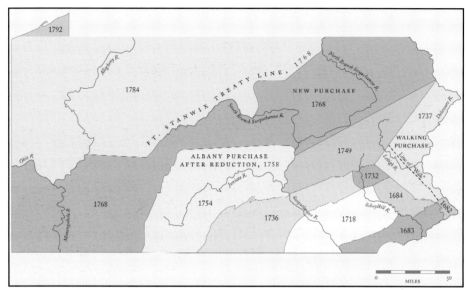

Iroquois Six Nations land cessions to Pennsylvania, 1736-1792 (claims of other Native nations excluded). Revised by Adrienne Gruver from Paul A. W. Wallace, *Indians in Pennsylvania*, rev. ed. (Harrisburg, 1981).

the travesty of 1737. He found vocal allies in the colony among Quaker political opponents of the proprietors. Other Delawares followed Nutimus to new homes in the Susquehanna valley. Still others went to the Ohio country, where they would nurse grudges against both the government of Pennsylvania and the Six Nations—and watch as more and more German and Scots-Irish immigrants took up lands in their midst. The Forks Delawares were not the only ones dispossessed by the diplomatic maneuvers of the Penn family government and its Iroquois allies. Two additional treaties between Pennsylvania and the Six Nations—at Philadelphia in 1749 and at the Albany Congress of 1754—transferred title to vast additional territories without the consent of the diverse Indians who lived there. Pennsylvania diplomacy triumphed on paper, but at the cost of destroying any legitimacy for the province's claim to William Penn's dream of "kind, just, and peaceable" relations.

Chapter 5
Race Wars, 1754-1794

Nothing could have been more alien to William Penn's vision than the comments of Major General Edward Braddock in 1755. When an Ohio country Delaware leader named Shingas offered his assistance to the general's campaign against Fort Dusquesne, which the French had constructed at the confluence of the Allegheny and Monongahela a year earlier, Braddock curtly declared that "No savage should inherit the land."[15] Needless to say, neither Shingas nor any significant number of Native Americans joined Braddock's army as it marched toward its ignominious defeat. "He looked upon us as dogs, and would never hear any thing what was said to him," an Ohio country Iroquois spokesman complained. "That was the reason that a great many of our warriors left him and would not be under his command."[16]

From the perspective of Delawares, Shawnees, and the many other Indian peoples who still clung to homes in the three watersheds of Pennsylvania, the first half of the eighteenth century had seen the steady eclipse of their status as "true lords of the soil." By going over local leaders' heads to deal solely with the Six Nations, Logan and Penn's sons had denied that Native people had any claim at all to the lands on which they lived apart from those granted by their supposed Iroquois overlords. Braddock's campaign threatened to take the logic to its final extreme. Bypassing both the Six Nations and the Pennsylvania proprietors, global imperial forces seemed to deny that *any* "savage" had rights to the land.

*   *   *

Both Braddock's expedition and the French construction of Fort Duquesne were, of course, products of a geopolitical rivalry directed from far-away imperial capitals. But the interest of the British and French empires in the Ohio country was itself a response to developments on the ground during the first half of the eighteenth century. Over the decades, a variety of Indian peoples had resettled the region—a region, that, it should be recalled, had never been connected by any geographical logic to the Susquehanna or Delaware watersheds and that had been largely depopulated at the end of the seventeenth century. Shawnees whose ancestral territories may have lain to the southwest, Wyandots who lived to the northwest and granted permission for some of the Indian newcomers to settle lands there, and Six Nations Iroquois who lived to the north and asserted rights of conquest had, of course, far stronger claims than any Europeans to the land—but all were newcomers to their particular villages, and all jostled for control in an arena of extraordinary ethnic and political complexity. Traders from Pennsylvania followed the Indian migrants from the Delaware and Susquehanna into their new homes and were soon joined by rivals from Virginia. Their activities attracted the attention of land speculators, their respective provincial governments—and the government of New France.

In 1749, alarmed by what it rightly perceived as British schemes for expansion west of the Appalachians and threats to the French network of Native trading alliances, the governor of New France sent an expedition from Montreal through the Ohio country to Detroit under the command of Pierre-Joseph Céloron de Blainville. Far from rallying Indian trading partners to the Gallic cause, the expedition alienated those concerned about rights to their

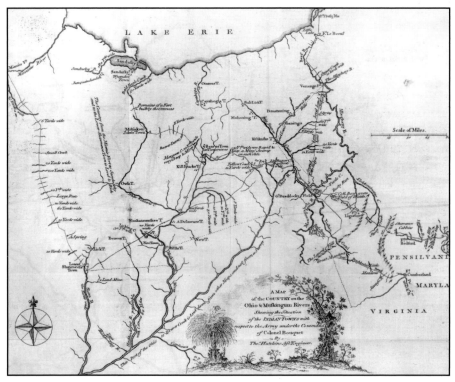

Map of the Ohio country in the 1760s. From [William Smith], *An Historical Account of the Expedition Against the Ohio Indians, in the Year MDCCLXIV* (Philadelphia, 1766). *Annenberg Rare Book and Manuscript Library, Van Pelt-Dietrich Library Center, University of Pennsylvania, Philadelphia.*

lands when it made a great show of hanging metal plaques on trees and bury-
ing lead plates at strategic spots to assert Louis XV's claims. In subsequent
years, the French pressed their assertions with a chain of posts that would cul-
minate with the establishment of Fort Duquesne. Although many of the
region's Indian inhabitants at least begrudgingly welcomed the French as an
alternative source of trade goods and a counterbalance to British power, others deeply resented them. As a result, in 1754, when Virginia Governor Robert
Dinwiddie sent a troop of militia under George Washington to halt construction at Fort Duquesne, some Ohio Indians welcomed the intrusion. Indeed,
the Ohio Iroquois Tanaghrisson struck the crucial blow against the French in
what nonetheless turned out to be a humiliating defeat for Washington.
Braddock and his supposedly crack troops had been sent from the British Isles
to complete the job the Virginians had started.

These events were the beginnings of the global imperial conflict that
came to be known in Europe as the Seven Years War. Among North
Americans, it has more commonly been called "the French and Indian War,"
a title that—with its assumption that all Native Americans joined with the
French against the British and their colonies—is not strictly accurate. Many of
the Iroquois Six Nations, some other Native Americans, and even a handful of
people of the Susquehanna and Ohio countries fought alongside the British,
and most of the Indians who fought beside the French did so for their own reasons, rather than at the bidding of an imperial power with which they allied
for convenience. Nonetheless, the term "French and Indian War" does convey
a broader perceptual truth about Anglo-American understandings. By the end
of the conflict, most Pennsylvania Euro-Americans assumed that *all* Indians
were their enemies. And most Indians returned the favor. The racial hatred
and bloodshed would continue almost without pause right through the period
of the War for Independence until, by the mid-1790s, only a handful of
Indians remained within the boundaries of the new Commonwealth of Pennsylvania.

*   *   *

When fighting between the French and British empires began, for most of the
Indians of the Susquehanna and Ohio countries, the choice should have been
plain. Braddock's arrogance (and military ineptitude); decades of embittered
experiences as the government of Pennsylvania pushed them from homes in
the east; distrust of the Iroquois Six Nations who had consented to their dis-
possession—all presented a compelling case for the French as the least distaste-
ful option. As a spokesman for one of the Native allies of New France put it
in 1754,

Brethren, are you ignorant of the difference
between our [French] Father and the English?
Go see the forts our Father has erected, and
you will see that the land beneath his walls is
still hunting ground, having fixed himself in
those places we frequent, only to supply our
wants; whilst the English, on the contrary, no
sooner get possession of a country than the
game is forced to leave it; the trees fall down
before them, the earth becomes bare, and we
find among them hardly wherewithal to shel-
ter us when the night falls.[17]

An Ohio country
orator reading
wampum belt.
From [William
Smith], *An
Historical Account of
the Expedition
Against the Ohio
Indians, in the Year
MDCCLXIV*
(Philadelphia,
1766). *Annenberg
Rare Book and
Manuscript Library,
Van Pelt-Dietrich
Library Center,
University of
Pennsylvania,
Philadelphia.*

Yet war is seldom simple. The same intrusion of Scots-Irish and German settlers into the west that was such a major grievance also meant that many Euro-Americans had deep personal ties with Indians. Some had settled at Indian invitation and even paid rent for their land. Mutual trading, drinking, and eating occurred in countless cabins. Moreover, many Indians had spent time with Moravian or other missionaries, been baptized, and bore Christian as well as Native names. Dozens still lived within the bounds of the Walking Purchase at Moravian Gnadenhütten ("Huts of Grace") and elsewhere. In and outside the missions, Indian and non-Indian people used many of the same material goods, hunted in the same woods with the same kinds of weapons, spoke the same Germanic-, Celtic-, or Algonquian-inflected English tongue. As one young man recalled, the Native Americans who captured him "mostly all spake English, one spake as good English as I can."[18] The war was deeply personal.

And therefore bloodily brutal. As late-twentieth-century Bosnia and Rwanda demonstrated, ethnic conflicts can become most ruthless when the parties have long lived side-by-side and know each other well. Precisely *because* the antagonists share personal histories, it apparently becomes necessary to dehumanize the enemy in the starkest ways, to draw clear and uncrossable lines between an *us* and a *them* that had long been blurred. When Delawares, Shawnees, and others took up arms, therefore, they did not engage in random acts of violence or broad strategic sweeps. Instead, they struck very specific targets, in particular homesteads of Euro-Americans who had settled on the lands the Six Nations had sold out from under them in the Walking Purchase and in the treaties of 1749 and 1754. Often they attacked people whose names they knew and against whom they had specific grievances. Corpses were not just scalped in accordance with long tradition, but often brutally mutilated in ways that were both morally transgressive expressions of rage and symbolic messages to those who would discover the devastation.

Euro-Americans returned the violence in kind—scalping Indian women and children, desecrating corpses, venting revenge for what they had seen done to their neighbors and kin—but seemed to do so in less focused ways, finding *any* Native American an appropriate target. In a way, the random brutality was a perversely unintended byproduct of Pennsylvania's history of Quaker pacifism. Although prominent Quakers had resigned from public participation in government in 1755, allowing the provincial assembly for the first time to vote funds to build frontier forts, raise troops, and supply arms— Pennsylvania's lack of any existing military infrastructure or supervised system of local militia forced western settlers to devise their own cruder, ad hoc, means of striking back. A bounty the provincial government offered for each Indian scalp validated the pattern. Yet the sources of brutality ran deeper, drawing on the same wells of personal knowledge of the enemy that infected Native

Americans. Ironically, the personal nature of the violence made those Indians who professed to be friends of Pennsylvania—Christians who lived with the Moravians, the handful of seemingly innocent people at Conestoga—especially suspect. Had not other Indians who had visited Euro-American homes, spoken German or English, and worn imported clothes turned out to be killers? So the frontiers of a colony founded by pacifists became killing fields.

A few on either side tried to remain above the general carnage, but those who advocated peace were vilified and pressured to choose. After repeated threats, the forty or so Christian Indians who remained at Moravian Gnadenhütten had to flee to Bethlehem in late 1755 when Delawares burnt the mission to the ground. Among Euro-Americans, the Moravians—like Quakers, pacifists—became increasingly suspect for their sheltering of Indians and their unwillingness to fight. Similarly, Israel Pemberton and other prominent Philadelphia Quakers, who formed a "Friendly Association for Regaining and Preserving Peace with the Indians by Pacific Measures" that often worked at cross-purposes to the proprietary government, earned the scorn of many non-Quaker colonists.

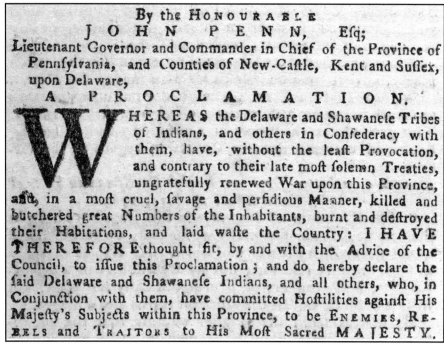

By the HONOURABLE

J O H N   P E N N,   Efq;

Lieutenant Governor and Commander in Chief of the Province of Pennfylvania, and Counties of New-Caftle, Kent and Suffex, upon Delaware,

A   P R O C L A M A T I O N.

WHEREAS the Delaware and Shawanefe Tribes of Indians, and others in Confederacy with them, have, without the leaft Provocation, and contrary to their late moft folemn Treaties, ungratefully renewed War upon this Province, and, in a moft cruel, favage and perfidious Manner, killed and butchered great Numbers of the Inhabitants, burnt and deftroyed their Habitations, and laid wafte the Country: I HAVE THEREFORE thought fit, by and with the Advice of the Council, to iffue this Proclamation; and do hereby declare the faid Delaware and Shawanefe Indians, and all others, who, in Conjunction with them, have committed Hoftilities againft His Majefty's Subjects within this Province, to be ENEMIES, REBELS and TRAITORS to His Moft Sacred MAJESTY.

Government proclamation announcing the payment of bounties to the civilians who took Delawares or Shawnees prisoner or killed them and turned in their scalps as evidence, 1764. The payment for the scalp of a male over ten years of age was $134; for female, $50. *Pennsylvania Gazette*, 12 July 1764. *Annenberg Rare Book and Manuscript Library, Van Pelt-Dietrich Library Center, University of Pennsylvania, Philadelphia.*

Nonetheless, heroic efforts by the Friendly Association, the Moravian missionary Christian Frederick Post, and the Delaware leader Pisquetomen patched together a truce by 1758—a truce greatly encouraged by French set-backs on the battlefield. In October of that year, at the Treaty of Easton, the Pennsylvania government agreed to prohibit further Euro-American settle-ment west of the Appalachians and to surrender much of the western land acquired in the 1754 Albany purchase. Significantly, however, those lands were returned to the Six Nations, not to the Delawares and other Indians who lived on them and who had fought so hard to regain them.

*   *   *

The Treaty of Easton was just a hiatus. On both sides, racial hatred smol-dered, and violence was never far from the surface. For years in the war-scarred Indian communities of the Susquehanna and Ohio countries, religious prophets had been preaching a message that stressed a pan-Indian identity that transcended ethnic and linguistic differences. Already a few years before Braddock's campaign, Presbyterian missionary John Brainerd heard the core of the message. It had been revealed to a young woman in a trance

> that the great God first made three men and three women, viz.: the Indian, the negro, and the white man. That the white man was the youngest brother, and therefore the white people ought not to think themselves better than the Indians. That God gave the white man a book, and told him that he must wor-ship him by that; but gave none either to the Indian or negro, and therefore it could not be right for them to have a book, or be any way concerned with that way of worship. And, furthermore, they understood that the white people were contriving a method to deprive them of their country in those parts, as they had done by the sea-side, and to make slaves of them and their children as they did of the negroes.[19]

By the early 1760s, this race-like doctrine of "separate creations" found new militance in the teachings of a man named Neolin, whom Euro-Americans called "The Delaware Prophet." Many of Neolin's disciples

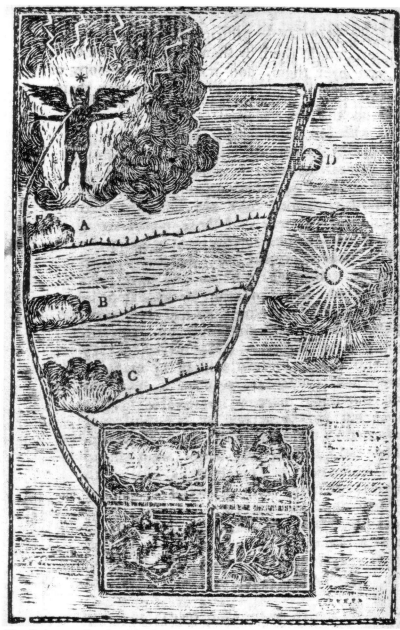

The Delaware Prophet Neolin's chart of his teachings, as reproduced from memory by Pennsylvanian John M'Cullough after his captivity during Pontiac's War. The path on the left leads to hell; the one on the right, to heaven, by way of a shining mountain. From Archibald Loudon, *A Selection of Some of the Most Interesting Narratives of the Outrages Committed by the Indians in Their Wars with the White People* (Carlisle, Pa., 1808-1811). *The Library Company of Philadelphia.*

believed that North America was meant solely for Indians. "As to those who come to trouble your lands—drive them out, make war upon them," the Master of Life supposedly told Neolin in a vision. "I do not love them at all; they know me not, and are my enemies, and the enemies of your brothers. Send them back to the lands which I have created for them and let them stay there."[20]

Neolin's message took on ever greater appeal after British forces defeated the French at Quebec in 1759, for it quickly became apparent that pledges made to Indians during the war meant little. As late as 1762, Delawares had been assured that "the English have no intention to make settlements in your hunting country beyond the Allegheny hills, unless they shall be desired for your conveniency to erect store houses in order to establish and carry on a trade."[21] Yet the British army dug into a string of posts from Fort Pitt (which replaced Duquesne) to Detroit to Michilimackinac, and squatters

The German bleeds & bears ye Furs | Th Hibernian frets with new Disaster | But help at hand Resolves to hold down
Of Quaker Lords & Savage Curs | And kicks to fling his broad brim'd Master | Th Hibernians Head or tumble all down

An anti-Indian and anti-Quaker cartoon by Henry Dawkins published in Philadelphia in 1764 conveys the level of racial hatred that prevailed at the time of the Conestoga Massacre. The caption reads "The German bleeds & bears the Furs / of Quaker Lords & Savage Curs / The Hibernian frets with new Disaster / And kicks to fling his broad brim'd Master / But help at hand Resolves to hold down / The Hibernians' Head or tumble all down." *The Library Company of Philadelphia.*

crossed the mountains into Indian country at the first opportunity. Meanwhile, the commander-in-chief of British forces, Sir Jeffrey Amherst, placed severe restrictions on commerce with Indians in the Ohio country and Great Lakes and made it clear that he had no intention of negotiating with Indians or following traditional customs of diplomacy.

The result was the violence of what is usually termed "Pontiac's War." Pontiac—an Ottawa war chief who was one of Neolin's adherents—had no direct influence outside his own region near Detroit, to which he laid siege for several months. In the Ohio and Susquehanna countries, Indians may have derived inspiration from Pontiac's activities, but they fought independently, and, essentially, resumed the war that had been put on hold at Easton a few years earlier. Their immediate provocation seems to have been the murder, by persons unknown, of Teedyuscung, in an April 1763 arson attack on the house the Pennsylvania government had built for him in the Wyoming Valley.

Euro-Americans responded to the Indian renewal of violence in kind—and the Conestoga massacre a few months after Teedyuscung's murder can be seen as simply a particularly gruesome example of the racial brutality that had become all too familiar in the past decade. Indeed, against the background of the Seven Years War, the slaughter of a defenseless community of Indians who professed to be friends of the provincial government and treasured their memories of the Quaker William Penn seems almost predictable. And so it went for a generation. Some years would be bloodier than others, marked by a few brutal murders on either side rather than all-out slaughter, but everywhere in the Susquehanna and Ohio countries, race war became the norm.

*   *   *

In 1764 and 1765, the heat of Pontiac's War gave way to another period of fragile cold war. Forces under Henry Bouquet reestablished British military supremacy; more important, under Amherst's replacement, Thomas Gage, and imperial Superintendent of Indian Affairs William Johnson, the British returned to a policy based on diplomacy rather than dictation. The Royal Proclamation of 1763 and a treaty signed at Fort Stanwix in 1768 committed the imperial government to the principle of a boundary separating British lands in the east from territories guaranteed to Indians in the west.

To Delawares, Shawnees, and others who lived in those territories, it was better than nothing, but the treaty must have seemed distressingly familiar. The "Line of Property" defined at Fort Stanwix yielded more than twice as much territory as had the detested Albany cession of 1754—including, by some interpretations, the entire southwestern quarter of today's Pennsylvania.

Just as familiarly, the deal was made between British governors and the Six Nations, with little participation by Ohio country Indian residents. Equally non-participating were the Euro-Americans who again flooded into the region west of the mountains and could not have cared less where imperial officials drew their boundary lines—particularly during the very years when a variety of issues (not least of them the Proclamation of 1763) was making imperial authority itself increasingly unpopular.

When colonial resistance to imperial authority turned the corner to revolution, the race war burst into the open again. This time, the European ally that Ohio country Indians reluctantly embraced was the British. The region's people of European stock who claimed for themselves the name "American," meanwhile, fought primarily—and brutally—not so much against the British as against the same Indian foes they had been battling for twenty years. Once again, on both sides, those who tried to bridge the racial divide found little ground on which to stand. Loyalist Euro-Pennsylvanians such as Simon Girty who lived with and fought beside Indians became legendary embodiments of unnatural "savagery," although their deeds were no worse than those of countless others on the rebel side.

As in earlier episodes, Moravians of either race were perhaps the most distrusted of all. After Pontiac's War, Moravian missionaries and their surviving Indian followers had moved west to establish three villages in the Muskingum valley of today's state of Ohio; one was called Gnadenhütten, in memory of the "Huts of Grace" earlier destroyed in the Lehigh valley. In late 1781, a party of Wyandot warriors tried to convince the Moravians to move to the British-allied Indian population centers on the Sandusky River. When they refused, the Wyandots briefly seized their missionaries, John Heckewelder and David Zeisberger, as captives and then forced everyone to abandon their

Moravian missionary John Heckewelder was one of the few Europeans who tried to bridge the late-eighteenth-century racial divide. Portrait by Gustav Anton von Senckendorff, c. 1822-1823. *American Philosophical Society.*

homes and relocate to the Sandusky. After nearly starving through the winter, some of the Indians returned to the Muskingum to harvest the corn they left standing in their fields before their relocation. Shortly thereafter, a militia from Washington County, Pennsylvania, herded 42 men, 20 women, and 34 children into two houses at Gnadenhütten, where they bludgeoned each of them to death.

*   *   *

The U.S. victory at Yorktown in 1781 and the Treaty of Paris in 1783 had almost no impact at all on the regional violence, which continued virtually without pause until Anthony Wayne's victory at Fallen Timbers in Ohio in 1794 and the subsequent Greenville Treaty of 1795. The latter drew a new boundary between Euro-American and Native American lands far to the west of Pennsylvania. The same Federal effort to settle boundaries that produced the Greenville Treaty—an agreement that most Indian participants accepted as legitimate—also produced negotiations between U.S. agent Timothy Pickering and the Six Nations at Canandaigua, New York, in 1794. The Canandaigua Treaty invalidated several controversial expropriations of lands by the state of New York, "described and acknowledged what lands belong to the Oneidas, Onondagas, Cayugas, and Senecas, and engaged [the Federal government] never to claim the same, nor to disturb them, or any of the Six Nations, or their Indian friends residing thereon, and united with them, in the free use and enjoyment thereof."[22] Yet none of the territory protected lay within Pennsylvania's boundaries.

The Treaty of Greenville, 1795, painted by a member of Anthony Wayne's staff. *The Chicago Historical Society.*

Chapter 6

Invisible Minorities, 1794-1918

In the decades after the Canandaigua Treaty, white Pennsylvanians rapidly consigned the state's remaining Native American population to a curious invisibility. That, despite the treaty's silence, a small group of descendants of the region's indigenous population would continue to live on a quasi-reservation within the state's boundaries receded from most Pennsylvanians' consciousness. That other Native people lived quietly among the general population received even less notice. Indians *outside* the state's boundaries, however, remained very much in the minds of some white Pennsylvanians. During the nineteenth century, Philadelphia became a leading center for national humanitarian organizations concerned with what many referred to as "the Indian problem," and Carlisle became the showpiece for Federal Indian education policies. Just as the late eighteenth-century violence of relations between Native people and Euro-Americans epitomized a much broader story, so too did Pennsylvania continue to embody developments of national significance.

*　　*　　*

The late eighteenth-century erasure of Pennsylvania's Native American population was all but complete. During the War for Independence, the interracial violence that everywhere scarred the landscape had been joined in 1779 by a systematic three-pronged assault by Continental troops under John Sullivan and James Clinton and Pennsylvania forces under Daniel Brodhead. The expeditions destroyed nearly every Indian village in the upper Susquehanna and Allegheny watersheds and central and western Iroquoia. Most inhabitants either fled westward into what became the state of Ohio or gathered as refugees at the British post of Niagara, from which many of their men conducted raids against the United States. After the Battle of Yorktown, many refugees returned to their former territories in what would become western New York. A smaller number—perhaps five hundred Senecas and a smaller group of Munsees—reoccupied sites around two Seneca hamlets along the Allegheny River that had escaped destruction during the war. The leading figure in the latter group was the Seneca chief Kayentwahkeh, also known as John O'Bail or Cornplanter.

　　When the war between Britain and the new nation was over, both the general government under the Articles of Confederation and the Commonwealth of Pennsylvania considered these and other Native

The Seneca Chief Kayentwahkeh (Cornplanter), painting by F. G. Bartoli, 1796. *Collection of The New-York Historical Society.*

Americans who had fought alongside the British (and, for that matter, many who had not) to be conquered people. In April 1783, John Dickinson, president of the state's Supreme Executive Council, argued that Congress should notify the Indians "that peace has been made with Great Britain . . . ; that the back country with all the forts is thereby ceded to us; that they must now depend upon us for their preservation and, that unless they immediately cease from their outrages . . . we will instantly turn upon them our armies that have conquered the king of Great Britain . . . and extirpate them from the land where they were born and now live."[23] At the same time, however, Pennsylvania officials continued to wrap themselves in the diplomatic mantle of William Penn. Although "we have full power to maintain our title by force of arms," Dickinson declared, "we sincerely intend to treat them, as our ancestors treated their forefathers, and to deal friendly with them, if they will suffer us to do so."[24]

At a series of treaties—at Fort Stanwix, New York, in 1784, Fort McIntosh on the Ohio River in 1785, Fort Finney on the Great Miami River in 1786, Fort Harmar on the Ohio in 1788—the U.S. government imposed peace on the Iroquois, the Delawares, the Shawnees, and major Ohio Valley and Great Lakes nations, treaties that the vast majority of these peoples regarded as illegitimate and that inspired the renewed warfare in the Ohio country that would continue until Fallen Timbers. Pennsylvania negotiators attended the Fort Stanwix and Fort McIntosh treaties and, in exchange for payments worth no more than about $7,000, acquired documents bearing a handful of Iroquois, Delaware, and Wyandot signatures transferring "all that part of the said commonwealth not yet purchased of the Indians within the acknowledged limits of the same"—everything, that is, except the "Erie Triangle," which would be purchased from the Confederation for approximately $150,000 in 1788 and from the Iroquois for approximately $1,000 at the Fort Harmar Treaty.[25]

The disparity between the prices the Pennsylvania government paid white and Indian claimants is only part of a complicated story. The negotiations—if that is the term for them—that Pennsylvanians carried out at Stanwix, McIntosh, and Harmar were sullied by mysteriously lost and misleading documents and contested memories of what Indian participants accepted. Throughout a sordid process that echoed the Walking Purchase, Cornplanter and other Seneca leaders fought valiantly to preserve something of their people's lands and other rights against the Pennsylvania juggernaut, insisting in particular that the agreement regarding the Erie Triangle explicitly protect the rights of Senecas to hunt and fish in the territory. These struggles—along with Cornplanter's efforts to broker peace between Pennsylvania and the Delawares and Shawnees—bore only modest fruit. In 1791, the commonwealth's government made a personal grant of approximately fifteen hundred acres in present-day Warren County to Cornplanter and his descendants, while also confirming the title of another Seneca chief named Great Tree to two islands in the Allegheny River.

For the better part of two centuries, these tiny plots of ground—legally private property rather than a tribal reservation—remained the only officially recognized Indian lands in Pennsylvania. Notably, even this slender recognition was limited to a group of Iroquois, excluding the Lenapes, Munsees, and Shawnees whose rights the Pennsylvania government had so long systematically ignored in favor of the Six Nations. Like Conestoga Manor before it, the "Cornplanter Tract" would be a tiny proprietary island in a vast hostile sea. The level of hostility became clear even before Cornplanter and his party returned home from Philadelphia after receiving title to the tract. Militiamen, reputedly from Virginia, attacked them just north of Pittsburgh and stole nearly everything they carried with them. Squatters and land surveyors, meanwhile, rapidly made a mockery of any hunting and fishing rights the Cornplanter Senecas were supposedly guaranteed in the Erie Triangle and places adjacent.

Indeed, as had been the case so often earlier in the eighteenth century, in this period Pennsylvania's relations with Indians had been driven relentlessly by the need to acquire title to real estate. Months before the Fort Stanwix Treaty, the Pennsylvania legislature had already declared most of the Indian territory south of the Allegheny River to be "Depreciation Lands," set aside to compensate war veterans for the financial losses inflation had inflicted on their pay. Plans were also underway to define the territory north of the river as "Donation Lands," to be granted in lieu of veterans' pensions. Thus the newly independent commonwealth remained deeply rooted in some of its worst traditions—even as Thomas Mifflin, the first governor under its revised constitution of 1790, proudly declared to an Indian delegation visiting Philadelphia that "the conduct of Pennsylvania, from the landing of William Penn to this day, has unequivocally proved *her* love of justice, *her* disposition for peace, and *her* respect for the rights and happiness of her neighbors."[26]

*   *   *

Two other, more admirable, Pennsylvania traditions also continued into the nineteenth century. In these dark times for Native Americans in the region, the pan-Indian spirit of religious revitalization that had flourished in the Susquehanna and Ohio valleys found new expression on the Cornplanter Tract and among the larger community of Allegany Senecas of New York State of which its people were a part. Clinging to tiny plots of land, cut off from realistic access to either old or new forms of livelihood, despised by their Euro-American neighbors, these communities were wracked with alcoholism and other social dysfunctions. Not surprisingly, among those most deeply affected were those who had lost the most—people such as Cornplanter's half-brother, the bearer of a hereditary chief's title that translates into English as "Handsome Lake," who apparently spent many of his days in a drunken stupor. *Prob drunk*

In June 1799, in a village on the Cornplanter Tract, Handsome Lake collapsed, apparently dead but actually in a coma, from which he later awoke to announce that he had been visited by messengers from the Creator. This and two subsequent visions, in August 1799 and February 1800, revealed what came to be known as the *Gaiwiio,* or Good Message. If Indian people were to avoid destruction, they must give up alcohol, witchcraft, "love-magic," and abortion—all of which the Creator deemed destructive of family and commu-

To pay its debts to Revolutionary War soldiers, in the mid-1780s, the Pennsylvania government hastened to acquire coerced title to Indian land west of the Allegheny River, to be granted to veterans as "Donation Lands" and "Depreciation Lands." Map from Joseph Henderson Bausman, *History of Beaver County, Pennsylvania and its Centennial Celebration* (New York, 1904). *Van Pelt-Dietrich Library Center, University of Pennsylvania Library.*

William Birch, *Back of the State House, Philadelphia* (1799), prominently features Indian visitors to the building now known as Independence Hall. In the minds of most white Pennsylvanians, Native Americans could now *only* be visitors in a state from which they had been almost entirely dispossessed. *Print and Picture Collection, The Free Library of Philadelphia.*

nity solidarity. They must also return to a traditional round of annual ceremonies. Over time, Handsome Lake increasingly emphasized the nuclear family rather than traditional bonds of lineage and clan and advocated a transformation of gender roles in which men would take up European-style plow agriculture and women abandon their corn fields for spinning and other new economic activities. In sum, the *Gaiwiio* sought to revitalize traditional religious beliefs and adapt them to what many saw as inevitable economic and social realities. In his own time and since, Handsome Lake's message was controversial among his compatriots, but the "New" or Longhouse Religion endures to this day as a central element in the persistence of Iroquois culture.

Quakers
st an Indian Committee

Among those who heard Handsome Lake's account of his visions were Quaker missionaries—bearers of a second colonial Pennsylvania tradition that continued to flourish through the nineteenth and into the twentieth century. As they had done since the days of the Walking Purchase, Quaker Pennsylvanians continued to speak out against abuses and, according to their best lights, to work on behalf of Indians. Building on the pre-revolutionary efforts of the Friendly Association, in 1795 the Philadelphia Yearly Meeting established an "Indian Committee" to coordinate its missions to Native Americans, a committee that survives to the present day. Quaker missions eschewed direct religious proselytization to concentrate instead on Euro-American-style literacy for youth, agriculture training for men, and domestic skills for women. All were quite controversial among Native Americans, for they represented direct assaults upon cultures that prized the oral transmission of knowledge and, still more fundamentally, upon ancient gendered patterns of labor, kinship, and domestic power relations. Nonetheless, in most early nineteenth-century Indian communities east of the Mississippi, leaders of some factions welcomed the concrete economic benefits of such activities, even as they rejected the assimilationist cultural assumptions on which they were based.

Quakers in Philadelphia—along with Friends in Baltimore, New York State, and elsewhere—justly earned reputations as members of a rare species: whites willing to give Native people a sympathetic ear. Philadelphia Friends in particular found themselves at the center of a circle of national reform groups deeply concerned with Indian affairs, most notably the Indian Rights Association, formed under the leadership of Philadelphians Herbert Walsh and Henry Pancoast in 1882, and the Lake Mohonk Conference of the Friends of the Indian, which began meeting at that New York resort in 1883. Quaker missions, meanwhile, focused increasingly on efforts outside the boundaries of the commonwealth—through the 1820s primarily among the Senecas of New York, and thereafter among peoples ever farther to the west.

*   *   *

To Friends, as well as to other white Pennsylvanians, Indians within the state boundaries remained largely invisible. The fragmentary and conflicting knowledge available even to experts is illustrated by ethnologist Henry Rowe Schoolcraft's encyclopedic compilation of *Information Respecting the History, Condition, and Prospects of the Indian Tribes of the United States*, published at Philadelphia between 1851 and 1855. A state-by-state table of figures from 1825 lists no Indian residents of Pennsylvania at all, yet a compilation of data from four years later estimates a population of 300 (locations and tribal affiliations are not listed). The same source reports that in 1847 eight families comprising 55 people lived on the Cornplanter Tract. The official U.S. government census did not even attempt to count Native Americans until 1860 and then, until 1890, enumerated only those "taxed"—that is, those who did not live on reservations. Pennsylvania tallied impossibly low totals of 7 persons in 1860, 34 in 1870, and 184 in 1880. The census-takers who did the classification—unable or unwilling to see an Indian presence in the commonwealth—no doubt pigeonholed some Native Americans as "white" and others as "black," depending on subjective perceptions of phenotype.

If the state's actual Native American residents remained largely invisible to the dominant population, more fanciful images of Indians remained very much a part of the culture—and not just in Hicks's images of the Peaceable Kingdom or in such widespread phenomena as cigar-store effigies and theatrical stereotypes. Long before the Revolution, Tamanend—the Lenape leader traditionally said to have participated in Penn's Treaty—had evolved into the legendary character who became the mythical forebear of the "Sons of St. Tammany" and countless similar organizations of (exclusively white male) Pennsylvanians who embraced pseudo-Indian identities and rituals. In 1849, the first of many Pennsylvania "tribes" of a middle-class fraternal organization known as "The Improved Order of Red Men" was established. Emblematic of the triumph of white imagination over Indian reality is the fact that, as late as 1990, a 1908 souvenir book produced by the organization was shelved in the reference section of the Pennsylvania State Library beside sources on genuine Native cultures. Also illustrative of nineteenth-century white Pennsylvania attitudes was the 1876 Centennial Exposition in Philadelphia, for which Spencer Fullerton Baird—a former professor at Pennsylvania's Dickinson College who was then an official of the Smithsonian Institution—planned an important exhibit on Native American life. Logistical problems, inter-agency feuding, insufficient funding, and poorly organized display cases ensured an exhibit that never seriously challenged visitors' beliefs that Indian cultures were relics of a bygone era.

*   *   *

All of these nineteenth-century embodiments of longstanding traditions—the primacy of stereotype over substance, the genuine humanitarian impulses of reformers who nonetheless sought to eradicate Indian cultures through assimilation into the dominant society, the pan-Indian experiences and movements so long rooted in the landscape—found their ultimate expression on Pennsylvania soil in the decades after the Civil War. In 1875, Richard Henry Pratt, a white Civil War veteran who had most recently commanded a troop

By the time the nation celebrated its centennial in Philadelphia in 1876, stereotypes of exoticism had replaced the state's original inhabitants in the popular
imagination. *Annenberg Rare Book and Manuscript Library, Van Pelt-Dietrich Library
Center, University of Pennsylvania, Philadelphia.*

making Indians into Americans

Pratt

of African American "Buffalo Soldiers" on the Great Plains, was posted to Fort Marion, Florida, to oversee seventy-two Indians held hostage for the good behavior of their Cheyenne, Kiowa, Comanche, and Caddo kin. Shortly after the prisoners arrived, Pratt removed the shackles they wore in the railroad cars that had brought them, gave them Euro-American style haircuts, dressed them in surplus military uniforms, and enlisted local women to begin teaching them to read. Over the next couple of years, Pratt gained a national reputation among both government officials and Quaker reformers for his educational efforts. In 1878 he took seventeen prized pupils to Virginia to establish an Indian division at Hampton Institute, the African American school established a decade earlier by fellow Civil War officer Samuel Chapman Armstrong.

At the same time, Pratt was developing more elaborate plans to open a separate institution, modeled after Hampton but devoted exclusively to Native Americans. He gained permission to use the abandoned army post of Carlisle Barracks for that purpose, and in September 1879 what later came to be called the Carlisle Indian Industrial Training School accepted its first eighty-two students. Pratt personally recruited (some might say kidnapped) most of this initial class from the Pine Ridge and Rosebud Lakota agencies in Dakota Territory. During the next four decades, over 10,000 young Native people from all over North America (and, ultimately, Puerto Rico and the Philippines) would follow them to the flagship of what became a system of Federal off-reservation boarding schools. Among approximately 8,600 Carlisle students whose tribal affiliations are specified (sometimes a bit idiosyncratically) in school records, the largest single contingent—1,776—came from the Iroquois Six Nations. These were joined by 75 Shawnees, 27 Delawares, and 3 Munsees—most of whom, despite their likely ancestral origins within Pennsylvania boundaries, probably came from the Indian Territory of today's Oklahoma. All told, nearly 4,400 students—roughly half of those identified— were from tribes with roots east of the Mississippi, including 2,600 whose people originated east of the Appalachians. Most of the easterners probably spoke English (for many, it was their first language) and had some elementary education before enrolling at Carlisle.

Nonetheless, in keeping with the stereotypes of the times, it was the rest of the student body—those from the Great Plains who seemed to conform to Victorian concepts of "savagery"—who predominated in both popular images of the school and, most importantly, in Pratt's rigorous educational philosophy, summed up in his famous motto, "Kill the Indian. . . and save the man."[27] Like nearly every white reformer of his day, Pratt firmly believed that the only hope for "the Indian" was total assimilation into the dominant culture, with its capitalist values and its generic Protestant morality. To "kill the Indian" was to obliterate every vestige of customs considered incompatible

The student body of the Carlisle Indian Industrial School, 1892. *Cumberland County Historical Society, Carlisle, Pa.*

with survival in the modern world—traditional languages, religions, folk beliefs, certainly economic patterns and modes of housing and dress—in order to save "the man" within from the destruction that otherwise would come inevitably from competition with the more "advanced" white race. Carlisle's location a thousand miles from the Great Plains was one of its greatest attractions. "To civilize the Indian, get him into civilization," Pratt was fond of saying; "To keep him civilized, let him stay."[28] Harsh as this philosophy was, it stood in stark contrast to the dominant evolutionary and Social Darwinist views of the day, which inclined to doom the entire Indian "race" to biological extinction, with little acknowledgment that a salvageable "man" might reside within.

Assimilationist dogma placed far more emphasis on behavioral and cultural indoctrination than on intellectual achievement. Indeed, the suspicion always lingered that Indians lacked intellectual capabilities suited to truly higher learning. At best, Carlisle Indian Industrial School students could achieve the equivalent of a tenth-grade education (no small achievement in an era when most white Americans went little farther than eighth grade). As the institution's official name suggests, the real emphases were on vocational training—relatively low-level crafts for boys, housekeeping for girls—that presumably would open the doors to productive citizenship, and of course on rigorous training in English language and Victorian morality. A distinguishing fea-

Sewing class, Carlisle Indian Industrial School. *Cumberland County Historical Society, Carlisle, Pa.*

ture of the Carlisle curriculum was the "Outing System," which placed students in private homes, often of Quaker families, during the summers. This served the triple purpose of preventing them from returning to the corrupting influences of their homes (most weren't even permitted to leave Pennsylvania to attend the funerals of parents), of furthering vocational and behavioral training, and (not least) of earning wages to finance a portion of their education and to support themselves.

Advanced as Carlisle was in terms of the reformist thinking of the day (and miserable as it was for the young people forced to undergo its fierce suppression of Native languages and its harsh assimilationist indoctrination), Pratt

Carpentry Shop, Carlisle Indian Industrial School. *Cumberland County Historical Society, Carlisle, Pa.*

Ninth-grade classroom, Carlisle Indian Industrial School, 1901. Note the various Native American artifacts. The questions on the blackboard pertain to Longfellow's *The Song of Hiawatha. Cumberland County Historical Society, Carlisle, Pa.*

had to struggle to maintain popular good will and government funding. He proved to be a master of public relations, by brilliantly playing upon both the positive and negative stereotypes in the minds of his constituents. Photography was central to Pratt's efforts, and carefully composed images of students' progress became staples of campaigns to raise financial and political support. Massed panoramas of well-scrubbed pupils; scenes of young men intently learning a craft; classroom shots of girls in Victorian dresses and boys in military uniforms studying (with no sense of irony) both patriotic themes and the pseudo-Indian history of Longfellow's *Hiawatha* joined individual portraits of apparently miraculous transformations from raw savagery to civilized propriety. What few viewers realized was that the before-and-after images were often taken on the same day—a hair cut, some new clothes, and some cues for proper posture did wonders—and that, in at least some cases, the photographic development process was deliberately manipulated to lighten skin tones in the "after" views to enhance the civilizing effect. Reform-minded audiences dreamed of savages turned into respectable citizens, and that is what they saw.

Reality was far more complex, and the degree to which students internalized the messages of cultural inferiority constantly thrown at them is difficult to determine. Certainly, for many students—particularly for those who came directly from the Great Plains with no English and little previous exposure to Euro-American culture—the experience was a wrenching ordeal. For eastern Indians who enrolled with some command of English (and who exchanged military uniforms not for blankets but for the same dungarees or calicoes that rural white Americans of the day wore), the ordeal must have been of a different sort, combining a fresh awareness of racism with conflicted attitudes toward being lumped together with people they may have also been inclined to see as "savages." But for an appalling number of students, the trauma was more basic. The 186 identical headstones that today stand in silent ranks in a cemetery near the grounds of the school are a solemn reminder of how many died as a result of disease, unfamiliar diet, and, to some indefinable degree, homesickness.

Still, many students who survived Carlisle left with mixed feelings. No one successfully completed the curriculum until 1889 (none of the original matriculates were among them). Perhaps ninety percent of those who did graduate remained in the East. Some went on to university and other higher education to become teachers, lawyers, or doctors—the core of a twentieth-century Native American professional class. Among these and others, literacy and other intellectual skills were deeply valued, and a variety of student newspapers and publications (albeit rigorously censored and part of Pratt's publicity apparatus) provided genuine outlets for creative expression. Perhaps most important, many of those who went to Carlisle—like those who, two centuries

Cemetery, Carlisle Indian Industrial School. *Photograph by Catherine Wert, 2003.*

earlier, gathered not far away in mixed villages of Shawnees, Delawares, and others—developed a powerful sense of pan-Indian identity. "There were kids who were Lakota, and there were kids who were Wampanoag," the school's most knowledgeable historian observes. "At Carlisle, they became Indian."[29]

This combination of professional and pan-Indian identity found its most prominent, and problematic, expression in an organization known as the Society of American Indians, founded in 1911 by a group of "Red

Progressives" that included Carlos Montezuma, the Yavapai physician who
had been the school's doctor in the 1890s, Zitkala-sa (Yankton Sioux), a
teacher at Carlisle, and alumni Charles Dagennett (Peoria) and Henry
Standing Bear (Lakota). Like its counterpart among African Americans, the
N.A.A.C.P. (founded in 1909), the S.I.A. preached both racial pride and
assimilation to the middle-class mainstream. Most of the organization's leaders shared, albeit uneasily, much of Pratt's condescension toward "blanket
Indians" and reservation life and so promulgated pan-Indian rather than tribal identity through the S.I.A.'s *American Indian Magazine* and, especially,
through promotion of an annual "American Indian Day" on June 22, "the
Moon of the First Fruits." (The holiday was officially celebrated for a time in
New York, Connecticut, and Wisconsin, but not Pennsylvania.) Disputes over
just how far assimilation should go, over whether to insist on the abolition of

Society of American Indians banquet, Philadelphia, 1914. *National Archives and Records
Administration, Washington, D.C.*

the Federal Bureau of Indian Affairs, and over whether such practices as the use of peyote in religious ceremonies could be tolerated led to the organization's demise in the early 1920s. Still, for all its faults and internal tensions, the S.I.A. had been the first genuinely Native-led organization to speak effectively for Indians within the broader political system. It would not be the last.

Nor, for the rest of the twentieth century, could the dilemmas of identity that wracked the Society of American Indians easily be resolved. "I felt that I was no more Indian, but would be an imitation of a white man," Luther Standing Bear, Henry Standing Bear's brother and one of Carlisle's most celebrated alumni, recalled. "And we are still imitations of white men, and the white men are imitations of the Americans."[30] Ironically, the ability of Carlisle students themselves to shape the contents of their identity as both "Indians" and "imitations of white men" increased as the institution began to stray from the original purity of Pratt's assimilationist vision. The school's founder had always been a thorn in the flesh of Federal bureaucrats—as early as his "Buffalo Soldier" days he had complained vociferously about corruption in

Backfield of the 1912 Carlisle Indian Industrial School football team: Alexander Arcasa, Stansil Powell, Gus Welch, Jim Thorpe (right). *Cumberland County Historical Society, Carlisle, Pa.*

the Bureau of Indian Affairs— and his controversies with superiors finally led to his ouster in 1904. Academically, Carlisle went into rapid decline, even as its reputation as an athletic powerhouse soared in the glory days of its legendary football coach Glenn S. "Pop" Warner and its greatest star, Jim Thorpe, who first enrolled in 1904. While Carlisle athletes inspired Native American fans all over the continent (and stimulated enrollments), the general climate of laxity allowed students to experiment in arts and other classes with genuine expressions of their cultural traditions. In some ways, then, the school's academic nadir may have been its apex as a seedbed of modern pan-Indian identity. Few government officials, of course, saw any of this as a good thing. In September 1918, although the school still enrolled approximately one thousand students, it fell victim to the army's need to return Carlisle Barracks to military use during World War I.

*   *   *

With the closing of Carlisle, Native Americans again became an invisible minority in the minds of non-Indian Pennsylvanians. Census figures again are revealing in their misleadingness. From high points of 1,639 in 1900 and 1,503 in 1910, the official number of Pennsylvania Native Americans plummeted erratically to 337 in 1920, 523 in 1930, and 441 in 1940. Just as revealing are the results of the 1950 census, the first in U.S. history in which people were allowed to specify their own racial classification. In an era when there was still nothing fashionable about embracing Native identity, Pennsylvania's enumerated Indian population suddenly almost tripled, to 1,141. Yet, even in the heyday of Carlisle, Native people had remained, in many respects, invisible to the commonwealth's dominant populations. Carlisle meant Jim Thorpe, Pop Warner, and Plains Indians who suddenly shed their blankets for proper military garb—not English-speaking Senecas and other eastern Indians who struggled against racism to seize the education denied them elsewhere. Throughout the nineteenth and early twentieth centuries, Native Americans' Pennsylvania, like the rest of the United States, was a profoundly hostile environment.

Chapter 7

Continuing Struggles, since 1918

Despite the small size of the state's Indian population, throughout the twentieth century the experiences of Pennsylvania's Native Americans continued to mirror national developments. The closing of the Carlisle Indian School coincided with what, in many respects, was the most depressing moment in the sad history of Federal relations with Native Americans. The Meriam Report, an officially commissioned study published in 1928, found appalling conditions everywhere in Indian country, with poverty, disease, and mortality rates many times higher than the national average. The report concluded that Federal assimilation policies, including those emphasizing off-reservation boarding schools, were primarily to blame. Calling for "more understanding of and sympathy for the Indian point of view," the authors hoped officials would "recognize the good in the economic and social life of the Indians in their religion and ethics and . . . seek to develop it and build on it rather than to crush out all that is Indian . . . in part because of the good it will do the Indians in stimulating a proper race pride and self respect."[31]

Informed by such thinking, "the Indian New Deal" of the 1930s dramatically changed the course of Federal policy. The worst excesses of assimilationist policies yielded to a substantial degree of tribal self-government and encouragement of cultural self-expression and religious freedom—albeit on terms too often dictated by Washington rather than designed by Indian people themselves. Like much of the New Deal, these policies came under attack in the 1950s, when the Eisenhower administration advocated the "termination" of reservations in the name of extending full civil rights to Native Americans. But this same policy shift also endorsed the Indian Claims Commission, a Federal entity long advocated by Native American leaders and created by Congress in 1946 to resolve, once and for all, financial and territorial obligations arising from historically violated treaty obligations. Nationally, by 1978 when the Commission was dissolved, nearly five hundred Native groups received compensation totaling $669 million.

More important than the financial compensation was the political and cultural opportunity the Indian Claims Commission presented for Native people throughout the country to seize the initiative, to research their own histories, to insist on what was due to them—and, in the process, to reinvigorate their collective identity and traditions. More than the top-down Indian New Deal, the Indian Claims Commission provided a framework within which a grass-roots Native renaissance became possible, and which, in the turbulent political climate of the 1960s and 1970s, would produce what was sometimes called the "Red Power" movement. As a new century dawned, indigenous peoples throughout eastern North America were far more assertive and self-confident in their cultural identity than at any time since the eighteenth century. But their economic and political status was, if anything, more contested, both internally and with respect to non-Indians, than ever.

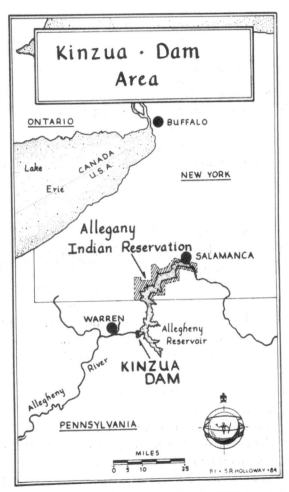

The Kinzua Dam project, which in 1966 flooded the Cornplanter Tract. Map by S. R. Halloway, *courtesy of Laurence M. Hauptman.*

*   *   *

Through these ups and downs of Federal policies and Native cultural revival, the small community that continued to live on the Cornplanter Tract came to play a much bigger role than their numbers could have predicted. As had been the case for ten thousand years, the waterways that defined Pennsylvania's human geography remained central to their story. For much of the first half of the twentieth century, Federal and state government planners dreamed of controlling the periodic flooding of the Allegheny River that brought devastation to Pittsburgh and to its surrounding steel mill communities. "Flood control," hydroelectric power, and recreational activities on artificial lakes all combined, in an era with environmental sensibilities quite different from those of a later generation, to produce a powerful set of arguments for redesigning the landscape. By the 1940s, dams and locks had tamed much of the Monongahela and Allegheny watersheds. In the 1950s, the Eisenhower administration, Pennsylvania governors George Leader and David Lawrence, and the U.S.

Protest against construction of the Kinzua Dam, early 1960s. *Courtesy of the Buffalo and Erie County Historical Society.*

Army Corps of Engineers pushed for completion of the scheme's crowning jewel, the Kinzua Dam, which would turn twenty-five miles of the Allegheny at the Pennsylvania-New York border into a reservoir and boating lake.

And inundate some nine thousand acres of Seneca land, including the entire Cornplanter Tract, along with much of the Allegany Reservation in New York State, condemned under the government's power of eminent domain. The homes of 130 Indian families (including some 200 people who lived on the Cornplanter Tract), cemeteries interring generations of ancestors, and such important sites as the Cold Spring Longhouse, long an important religious and cultural center for the followers of Handsome Lake, would be destroyed or flooded. The peculiar legal status of the Cornplanter Tract under Pennsylvania law made it particularly vulnerable, but the portion of the dam's "take area" in New York State clearly fell under the protection of the Canandaigua Treaty of 1794. Despite well-publicized protests by the Senecas themselves, by national Indian rights groups, by the Indian Committee of the Philadelphia Yearly Meeting, and by such articulate literary voices as Edmund Wilson—whose 1960 book, *Apologies to the Iroquois*, took up the cause—the government forged ahead with its plans to relocate the Senecas to two suburban housing developments built for them in western New York.

In 1964, on the eve of the dam's completion, Congress belatedly awarded the Senecas $15 million in compensation for their lost lands, but nothing could atone for the sense of cultural loss and personal devastation those affected endured. As one man said twenty years later, "My mind and . . . heart still hurt."[32] River waters had created the land of Indian Pennsylvania. In 1966, when the Kinzua Dam was completed, river waters destroyed it—but these were deliberately unleashed on behalf of the economic interests of non-Indians. Perhaps no single event in the state's history—not even the Conestoga Massacre—so eloquently symbolizes the tragic history of American Indians' Pennsylvania.

*   *   *

Yet that history no more ended in 1966 than it did in 1763. In Iroquoia and across the nation, the Kinzua affair was a galvanizing moment. Perhaps no single event prior to the Second Battle of Wounded Knee in 1973 did more to mobilize and then radicalize Native American activists. The American Indian Chicago Conference of 1961—a gathering of some 420 delegates from 67 tribes whose "Declaration of Indian Purpose" played a trail-blazing role in the "Red Power" movement analogous to that of the 1962 Port Huron Statement among students of the New Left—found major inspiration in the protests against Kinzua. Meanwhile, a young generation of Iroquois activists galvanized by events on the Cornplanter Tract played increasingly visible leadership roles both nationally in the American Indian Movement and internationally in a variety of campaigns for indigenous rights and sovereignty.

The same period that saw the destruction of the last Native land base within the state and the renewed national symbolic importance of what happened to Native people in Pennsylvania saw a significant expansion in the modest numbers of state residents who identified themselves as American Indians, from 2,122 in 1960 to 5,553 in 1970, 9,476 in 1980, 14,733 in 1990, and 18,348 in 2000. No doubt, the increases were partly due to cultural changes that led more and more people to embrace proudly an Indian identity that might, in earlier years, have been hidden in response to racial bigotry or submerged among a variety of ethnic heritages. But as with the Kinzua affair, the population increases also reflect broader Federal government policies of the mid-twentieth century. In the 1950s and 1960s, the government encouraged Native people to leave impoverished western reservations in search of economic opportunities in urban areas. The majority went to Phoenix, Los Angeles, Chicago, or other places nearer their homes, but Pittsburgh and Philadelphia, too, became home to growing numbers of young Indians struggling to makes ends meet and to maintain their diverse cultural traditions. By 2000, Philadelphia County had, by far, the largest Native American population in the state, with 4,073. Allegheny County—Pittsburgh—had the second largest, 1,593.

Grassroots Indian political organizations and community centers emerged in both cities and battled the twin problems of meager government funding and tensions among people of diverse backgrounds and relationships to tribal traditions. In the 1980s and 1990s, one such organization—the United American Indians of the Delaware Valley—made major progress in mobilizing Native people in the Philadelphia area and in serving their social and economic needs. Its community center on Chestnut Street near Independence Hall proudly reestablished a visible Indian physical presence at the core of the state's cultural landscape. Hard economic times, controversies over who could and could not claim Native identity, bitter infighting, and allegations of financial improprieties, however, led to the collapse of the organization in the summer of 2001.

Outside of Philadelphia, as small Indian communities throughout the eastern states (and indeed throughout the nation) struggled to gain legal recognition of their existence from Federal and state governments, Lenape groups in Pennsylvania also fought to win legal recognition. As had been the case nationally, those battles involved bitter controversies, both internal and external. Internally, the battles centered on sorting out the claims of long-scattered people of Native descent from those sometimes disparaged as members of "the Wannabe Tribe." Externally—especially after the passage of the Federal Indian Gaming Regulatory Act of 1988—the struggles confronted non-Indian charges that groups seeking recognition did so only to gain the right to establish casinos or win other privileges denied to other Pennsylvanians. Legally, the struggles were further compounded by Pennsylvania legal traditions that, since the days of the Walking Purchase, had denied Lenapes any independent collective title to lands within the commonwealth.

While, at the turn of the twenty-first century, activism on legal, political, and social fronts often stumbled, a very different form of promoting indigenous values and expressing pan-Indian cultural identity flourished in locales throughout the state. Powwows—the celebrations of dancing, drum-

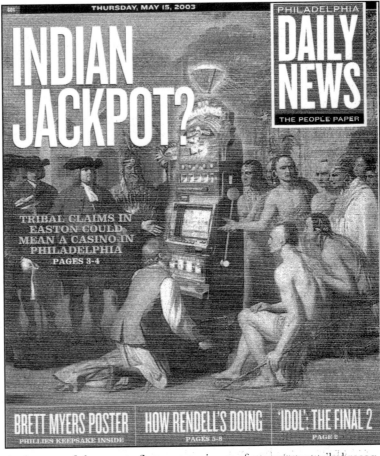

At the turn of the twenty-first century, issues of government tribal recognition invariably became intertwined with controversies over casino gambling on reservations. *Philadelphia Daily News*, 15 May 2003. *Reprinted by permission from The Daily News.*

Powwow, Carlisle, Pa., February 22, 2003. Photo by Pierce Bounds. *Courtesy of Dickinson College.*

ming, crafts, food, and cultural pride that united people from everywhere in Indian country—proliferated across the commonwealth. On at least one weekend a month in 2004, for instance, on fairgrounds or in fieldhouses scattered from Philadelphia to Pittsburgh, Tunkhannock to Titusville, and Clearfield to Carlisle, Indian people from across the continent gathered—and non-Indians learned about the significance of dancing in Native cultures, about the meanings of ceremonial regalia, and about the joys of eating frybread. In this most modern of Indian phenomena, many Native people in Pennsylvania found their most meaningful way of connecting to traditions long suppressed.

*   *   *

At the turn of the twenty-first century, as for nearly four hundred years, questions of contested space, of community boundaries, and of personal and cultural identity continued to define the terrain of Native Americans' Pennsylvania. Through the many millennia before the arrival of Europeans, there had never been a single Indian identity that embraced the varied peoples of the Delaware, Susquehanna, and Allegheny-Monongahela-Ohio watersheds. Only in the period of severe social and cultural disruption during the early eighteenth century did the first glimmerings of such a common identity appear, shaped by Native people themselves in response to the threats they perceived from the Pennsylvania government and Pennsylvania colonists who competed for the land. From the late eighteenth century to the present day, those other Pennsylvanians increasingly erased Native people from the landscape, sometimes violently, more often through legal and cultural fictions. Through it all, events in Pennsylvania—the Walking Purchase, the Conestoga Massacre, the post-Revolutionary land cessions, the Carlisle Indian School experience, the Kinzua Dam affair—revealed national trends in starkest relief. Native Americans' Pennsylvania has been, in microcosm, Native Americans' United States.

Notes

1. Francis Jennings, "'Pennsylvania Indians' and the Iroquois," in Daniel K. Richter and James H. Merrell, eds., *Beyond the Covenant Chain: The Iroquois and Their Neighbors in Indian North America, 1600–1800* (Syracuse, N.Y., 1987), 75.
2. Kathryn Jean Lopez, "James Carville on Bob Casey," *National Review Online*, June 1, 2000 <http://www.nationalreview.com/interrogatory/interrogatory060100.html>.
3. Robert Juet, "The Third Voyage of Master Henry Hudson," in J. Franklin Jameson, ed., *Narratives of New Netherland, 1609–1664* (New York, 1909), 18.
4. Albert Cook Myers, ed., *William Penn's Own Account of the Lenni Lenape or Delaware Indians*, rev. ed. (Wallingford, Pa., 1970), 35–36.
5. Adrian van der Donck, "Description of the New Netherlands," trans. Jeremiah Johnson [2d ed., 1656], *Collections of the New-York Historical Society*, 2d ser., vol. 1 (1841), 183.
6. Myers, ed., *William Penn's Own Account*, 39.
7. Quoted in Francis Jennings, *The Ambiguous Iroquois Empire: The Covenant Chain Confederation of Indian Tribes with English Colonies from Its Beginnings to the Lancaster Treaty of 1744* (New York, 1984), 243.
8. William Penn "to the Kings of the Indians," Oct. 18, 1681, in Richard S. Dunn and Mary Maples Dunn, eds., *The Papers of William Penn*, 2 (Philadelphia, 1982), 128–129.
9. John Heckewelder, *History, Manners, and Customs of the Indian Nations Who Once Inhabited Pennsylvania and the Neighbouring States*, ed.William C. Reichel (Philadelphia, 1876), 75.
10. James Logan to John Penn, Penn Papers, Official Correspondence, II, 21, Historical Society of Pennsylvania, Philadelphia.
11. James Logan to John Penn, Aug. 2, 1731, Logan Letter Books, II, 7, Historical Society of Pennsylvania.
12. Quoted in Jennings, *Ambiguous Iroquois Empire*, 324.
13. Quoted in Anthony F. C. Wallace, *King of the Delawares: Teedyuscung* (Philadelphia, 1949), 25.
14. [Samuel Hazard, ed.], *Minutes of the Provincial Council of Pennsylvania, from the Organization to the Termination of the Proprietary Government* (Harrisburg, Pa., 1838–1852), 4: 575–580.
15. Beverly W. Bond, Jr., ed., "The Captivity of Charles Stuart, 1755–57," *Mississippi Valley Historical Review*, 13 (1926), 63.
16. Hazard, ed., *Minutes of the Provincial Council*, 6: 589.
17. E.B. O'Callaghan and B. Fernow, eds., *Documents Relative to the Colonial History of the State of New-York, 10* (Albany, N.Y., 1858), 269.
18. Quoted in Jane T. Merritt, *At the Crossroads: Indians and Empires on a Mid-Atlantic Frontier, 1700–1763* (Chapel Hill, N.C., 2003), 178.
19. Thomas Brainerd, *The Life of John Brainerd, The Brother of David Brainerd, and His Successor as Missionary to the Indians of New Jersey* (Philadelphia, 1865), 234–235.
20. [Robert Navarre?], *Journal of Pontiac's Conspiracy*, ed. M. Agnes Burton, trans. R. C. Ford (Detroit, Mich., [1912]), 30.
21. Hazard, ed., *Minutes of the Provincial Council*, 8: 269.
22. "A Treaty between the United States of America and the tribes of Indians called the Six Nations," Nov. 11, 1794, *American State Papers: Indian Affairs*, 1 (Washington, D.C., 1832), 545.
23. Hazard, ed., *Pennsylvania Archives*, 1st ser., vol. 10 (Philadelphia, 1854), 45.
24. *Ibid.*, 54.
25. Copy of ms. deed from Six Nations to Pennsylvania, 23 Oct. 1784, Francis Jennings, et al., eds., *Iroquois Indians: A Documentary History of the Diplomacy of the Six*

Nations and Their League (Woodbridge, Conn.: Research Publications, 1985), microfilm reel 38.

26. *Minutes of the Supreme Executive Council of Pennsylvania, from Its Organization to the Termination of the Revolution*, 14 (Harrisburg, 1853), 404.
27. Quoted in David Wallace Adams, *Education for Extinction: American Indians and the Boarding School Experience, 1875–1928* (Lawrence, Kan., 1995), 52.
28. Richard Henry Pratt, *Battlefield and Classroom: Four Decades with the American Indian, 1867–1904*, ed. Robert M. Uitley (New Haven, Conn., 1964), 283.
29. Barbara Landis, quoted in Stephanie Anderson, "On Sacred Ground," *Central Pa. Magazine* (May 2000), 40.
30. Luther Standing Bear, *My People the Sioux*, ed. E. A. Brininstool (Lincoln, Neb., 1975), 141.
31. Institute for Government Research, *The Problem of Indian Administration* (Baltimore, 1928).
32. Quoted in Laurence M. Hauptman, *The Iroquois Struggle for Survival: World War II to Red Power* (Syracuse, N.Y., 1986), 85.

Suggestions for Further Reading

Historical writing on Native Americans in the region that became Pennsylvania has a long tradition that, until very recently, has, in an odd way, been both rich and impoverished at the same time. The richness stems from the fact that, in almost every generation from the early nineteenth through mid-twentieth centuries, one or two authors carefully mined the commonwealth's archives and oral traditions to reconstruct events in extraordinary detail, albeit in ways often colored by the racial biases of their day. The impoverishment stems from the facts that, apart from that handful of men, few scholars took the work seriously, that the work focused almost exclusively on the violent period from the Seven Years War through the U.S. War of Independence, and that other aspects of the Native experience (much less the voices of Native people themselves) received little attention.

The two earliest accounts are in many ways the richest, for they were written by Moravian missionaries who spoke Delaware, knew Native people well, and took a genuine interest in Indian oral traditions. John Heckewelder's *History, Manners, and Customs of the Indian Nations Who Once Inhabited Pennsylvania and the Neighbouring States*, first published in 1818 and republished as edited by William C. Reichel in 1876, is an invaluable source on Delaware customs and beliefs. The voluminous diaries of Heckewelder's colleague David Zeisberger contain a far fuller, if less digested, trove of information. Portions were collected by Archer B. Hulbert and William Nathaniel Schwarze as "David Zeisberger's History of Northern American Indians" and published in the *Ohio Archaeological and Historical Quarterly* (1910) and by Eugene F. Bliss as *Diary of David Zeisberger, a Moravian Missionary among the Indians of Ohio* (Cincinnati, 1885). An authoritative English edition of materials dealing with the period of the U.S. War of Independence is Hermann Wellenreuther and Carola Wessel, *The Moravian Mission Diaries of David Zeisberger, 1772–1781*, trans. Julie Tomberlin Weber (University Park, PA., 2005).

Subsequent nineteenth- and early twentieth-century chroniclers were much less sympathetic to Native points of view than were Heckewelder and Zeisberger, but despite obvious prejudices, their books, which remain in print, compile a mass of original source material, much of it not preserved elsewhere. In 1846 and 1847, Pittsburgh resident Neville B. Craig (who personally witnessed many of the events he wrote about) published a monthly series of documents and sketches entitled *The Olden Time*, subsequently reprinted as a two-volume set in 1876. Also deeply rooted in local lore were such books as H. Frank Eshleman's *Lancaster County Indians* (Lancaster, Pa., 1908); Charles A. Hanna's *The Wilderness Trail* (New York, 1911); C. Hale Sipe's *The Indian Chiefs of Pennsylvania* (Butler, Pa., 1927) and *The Indian Wars of Pennsylvania* (Harrisburg, 1929); and George P. Donehoo's *A History of the Indian Villages and Place Names in Pennsylvania* (Harrisburg, 1928). From this period, virtually the only dispassionate study that meets the standards of modern scholarship—and remains worth reading on its own terms—is Randolph C. Downes's *Council Fires on the Upper Ohio; A Narrative of Indian Affairs in the Upper Ohio Valley until 1795* (Pittsburgh, 1940).

Late nineteenth- and early twentieth-century anthropological and linguistic scholarship on Native peoples of the Pennsylvania region and their descendants was of much higher quality than most historical writing. Much of the work of such intellectual giants as University of Pennsylvania professor Frank G. Speck was highly technical and not particularly accessible to the general reader, but see Speck's *A Study of the Delaware Indian Big House Ceremony* (Harrisburg, 1931). Unfortunately far more accessible, and still widely available in reprint, is *The Lenâpé and Their Legends* (Philadelphia, 1885), by Daniel G. Brinton, an otherwise careful scholar who—like many others then and now—accepted the authenticity of a text known as the *Walam Olum*, a purported transcription of a pictographic record of the origins and migrations of the Lenape that was concocted in the 1830s by a colorful character named Constantine Samuel Rafinesque.

Bridging the intellectual worlds of earlier antiquarians and later academic scholarship are the prolific works of two mid-twentieth-century authors who combined the skills of ethnologists, oral historians, and archival researchers, although neither had advanced degrees in any of those fields. C. A. Weslager, in books such as *Delaware's Forgotten Folk: The Story of the Moors and Nanticokes* (Philadelphia, 1943), *The Delaware Indians: A History* (New Brunswick, N.J., 1972), *The Delaware Indian Westward Migration* (Wallingford, Pa., 1978), and *The Nanticoke Indians: Past and Present* (Newark, Del., 1983), burst out of the traditional emphases on conflict and on the eighteenth century to tell Native-centered human stories that stretched both far back in time and into the present. Similarly wide-ranging in interests was Paul A. W. Wallace, whose *The White Roots of Peace* (Philadelphia, 1946) made Iroquois traditions accessible to a wide audience, whose *Indian Paths of Pennsylvania* (Harrisburg, 1965) meticulously recreated a Native landscape, and whose *Indians in Pennsylvania* (Harrisburg, 1961, 2d rev. ed. by William A. Hunter, 1993) remains the only book-length general history.

Scholarship based in the academy began to flourish only in what was, quite literally, the next generation, with the work of Wallace's son, anthropologist Anthony F. C. Wallace. His *King of the Delawares: Teedyuscung, 1700-1763* (Philadelphia, 1949) and *The Death and Rebirth of the Seneca* (New York, 1969) remain masterpieces—beautifully written, thoroughly and imaginatively researched, and brimming with insights—and his many scholarly articles on religious revitalization movements, on gender, and on intersections of psychology and culture have had enormous impact on the interdisciplinary approach that came to be known as "ethnohistory." While the anthropologist Wallace worked through Pennsylvania Native topics (as well as many others) to develop theoretical tools, historian Francis Jennings brought Native American experiences forcefully into the mainstream of general scholarship on American history through intense archival work on Pennsylvania's troubled eighteenth-century relations with its Indian neighbors. His acerbic trilogy on the "Covenant Chain" alliance between the Iroquois and the English—*The Invasion of America* (Chapel Hill, N.C., 1975), *The Ambiguous Iroquois Empire* (New York, 1984), and *Empire of Fortune* (New York, 1988)—focuses relentlessly on the Penn family policies that dispossessed the Delawares and on the ideological devices that whitewashed so much of the Pennsylvania, and broader American, experience.

After Wallace and Jennings, the history of relations between Native

Americans and Euro-Americans in the Pennsylvania region ceased to be a lonely calling. Sophisticated and well-written scholarship has blossomed in recent years, with much more to come as recent Ph.D. students begin to revise their books for publication. The new work includes Peter C. Mancall, *Valley of Opportunity: Economic Culture along the Upper Susquehanna, 1700-1800* (Ithaca, N.Y., 1991); Gregory Evans Dowd, *A Spirited Resistance: The North American Indian Struggle for Unity, 1745-1815* (Baltimore, 1992); Michael N. McConnell *A Country Between: The Upper Ohio Valley and its Peoples, 1724-1774* (Lincoln, Neb., 1992); Eric Hinderaker, *Elusive Empires: Constructing Colonialism in the Ohio Valley, 1673-1800* (New York, 1997); James H. Merrell, *Into the American Woods: Negotiators on the Pennsylvania Frontier* (New York, 1999); Jane T. Merritt, *At the Crossroads: Indians and Empires on a Mid-Atlantic Frontier, 1700-1763* (Chapel Hill, N.C., 2003); and William A. Pencak and Daniel K. Richter, eds., *Friends and Enemies in Penn's Woods: Indians, Colonists, and the Racial Construction of Pennsylvania* (University Park, Pa., 2004).

One thing, though, has not changed: the vast majority of scholarship continues to focus on the eighteenth century and on conflict between Native people and colonists. The seventeenth century before the creation of Penn's colony has received much less attention. Here (and on many other periods and topics), the best sources are numerous articles in the commonwealth's two scholarly journals, *Pennsylvania History* (published since 1934) and *The Pennsylvania Magazine of History and Biography* (since 1877). Book-length studies focused on specific tribal groups remain surprisingly few. On the Delawares, in addition to Weslager's books, see W. W. Newcomb, *The Culture and Acculturation of the Delaware Indians* (Ann Arbor, 1956); Gladys Tantaquidgeon, *Folk Medicine of the Delaware and Related Algonkian Indians* (Harrisburg, 1977); Herbert C. Kraft, *The Lenape: Archaeology, History, and Ethnography* (Newark, N.J., 1986); and Robert Steven Grumet, *The Lenapes* (New York, 1989). On the Iroquois see Daniel K. Richter, *The Ordeal of the Longhouse: The Peoples of the Iroquois League in the Era of European Colonization* (Chapel Hill, N.C., 1992); Matthew Dennis, *Cultivating a Landscape of Peace: Iroquois-European Encounters in Seventeenth-Century America* (Ithaca, N.Y., 1993); Dean R. Snow, *The Iroquois* (Cambridge, Mass., 1994); and William N. Fenton, *The Great Law and the Longhouse: A Political History of the Iroquois Confederacy* (Norman, Okla., 1998). Far less scholarship exists on the Shawnees, but see James H. Howard *Shawnee! The Ceremonialism of a Native Indian Tribe and its Cultural Background* (Athens, Ohio, 1981)

On much earlier periods, Pennsylvania has a rich tradition of archaeological scholarship. Since its first publication in 1930, the journal *Pennsylvania Archaeologist* has compiled a treasure-trove of information by both professional and avocational archaeologists in every part of the state. Excellent surveys of archaeological discoveries may be found in Robert E. Funk and Bruce E. Rippeteau, *Adaptation, Continuity, and Change in Upper Susquehanna Prehistory* (George's Mills, N.H., 1977); Barry C. Kent, *Susquehanna's Indians* (Harrisburg, 1984); Jay Custer, *Prehistoric Cultures of Eastern Pennsylvania* (Harrisburg, 1995); and Kurt W. Carr and James M. Adovasio, eds., *Ice Age People of Pennsylvania* (Harrisburg, 2002). A brief introduction for the non-specialist is Kent's *Discovering Pennsylvania's Archeological Heritage*, rev. ed. (Harrisburg, 1994).

Not surprisingly, very little has been published on the experiences of Native Americans in Pennsylvania in their period of virtual invisibility after 1800. Perhaps the best general surveys of the period are a series of books by Laurence M. Hauptman on the Iroquois of neighboring New York State: *The Iroquois in the Civil War: From Battlefield to Reservation* (Syracuse, 1993); *The Iroquois and the New Deal* (Syracuse, 1981); and *The Iroquois Struggle for Survival: World War II to Red Power* (Syracuse, 1986). The Carlisle Indian School is explored in David Wallace Adams, *Education for Extinction: American Indians and the Boarding School Experience, 1875-1928* (Lawrence, Kan., 1995); Linda F. Witmer, *The Indian Industrial School: Carlisle Pennsylvania 1879-1918* (Carlisle, 1999); and in a web site maintained by Barbara Landis <http://home.epix.net/~landis/>. On white reformers, see Francis Paul Prucha, *American Indian Policy in Crisis: Christian Reformers and the Indian, 1865-1900* (Norman, Okla., 1976); William T. Hagan, *The Indian Rights Association: The Herbert Welsh Years, 1882-1904* (Tucson, Ariz., 1985); and Frederick E. Hoxie, *A Final Promise: The Campaign to Assimilate the Indians, 1880-1920* (Lincoln, Neb., 1984). Hazel W. Hertzberg, *The Search for an American Indian Identity: Modern Pan-Indian Movements* (Syracuse, N.Y., 1971) provides an introduction to the Society of American Indians. The Kinzua Dam affair and its enduring impact are the subject of Joy A. Bilharz, *The Allegany Senecas and Kinzua Dam: Forced Relocation through Two Generations* (Lincoln, Neb., 1998). A brief overview of current issues is provided by Troy Richardson in *Native Americans in Contemporary Pennsylvania* (Harrisburg, 1994).

This Publication is supported

by a grant from

the Pennsylvania Historical and Museum Commission

Other titles in
The Pennsylvania History Studies Series

Philadelphia: A Brief History, by Roger D. Simon
Pennsylvania Reformers, by Ira V. Brown
Pennsylvania's Decorative Arts, by Irwin Richman
Pennsylvania Painters, by Irwin Richman
The Quakers: A Brief Account of Their Influence on Pennsylvania, by William
W. Comfort
Pennsylvania Kingmakers, ed. by Robert G. Crist
Pennsylvania and the Federal Constitution, ed. by Robert G. Crist
Pennsylvania and the Bill of Rights, ed. by Robert G. Crist
The Iron Industry in Pennsylvania, by Gerald G. Eggert
Pennsylvania's Architecture (revised edition), by Irwin Richman

Ethnic Series

Scotch-Irish Presence in Pennsylvania, by James H. Smylie
The Black Presence in Pennsylvania: "Making It Home," second edition, by
Emma Lapsansky
Irish in Pennsylvania, by Dennis Clark
Polish Presence in Pennsylvania, by Matthew Magda
Jewish Life in Pennsylvania, by Dianne Ashton
The Pennsylvania Germans, revised edition, by Charles H. Glatfelter

To learn more about these titles and to place orders, visit the website
http://www.pa-history.org/pastudyseries.htm or contact The
Pennsylvania Historical Association, 108 Weaver Building, University
Park, PA 16802-5500